Authors' Note

You may be wondering why *Spelling Made Easy* would take up so many pages of a book. The fact is that spelling by this approach is *easy* if you take one simple step at a time in the right, logical order.

The programme has three distinct phases, and each phase has its own characteristics. When you have read the first section, which tells you how to begin, tackle each phase in turn, and master each section before going on to the next. As you go along you will see that the whole study fits together in an understandable and fascinating pattern.

In our experience students who have never previously managed to read and write successfully have, using this approach, made dramatic advances in spelling and reading in a matter of hours. Many pages are devoted to example words and practice lists to reinforce your understanding.

We wish all our readers stimulating and successful learning.

Spelling Made Easy

*Barbara Dykes &
Constance Thomas*

Hale & Iremonger

Acknowledgements

People of all ages, Australian born and migrants, who came to The Language Foundation of Australia for help with English spelling and reading provided much of the feedback required for this programme.

We acknowledge the work of Mrs Romalda Spalding, Dr Théodore MacDonald, Mr Tom Taylor, Mrs Joan Tucker, and Mrs Elsie Smelt, author of *Complete Guide to English Spelling*. Mrs Elsie Smelt's work with migrants, presenting the language in three clear sections, often brought the comment 'This makes sense of the English language at last!'

We also thank Gavin Swallow, now a Spelling Consultant in Brisbane and a Director of The Language Foundation of Australia, for his helpful ideas and untiring support.

© 1989 Barbara Dykes and Constance Thomas
10 9 8 7 6 5

This book is copyright. Apart from any fair dealing for the purposes of study, research, criticism, review, or as otherwise permitted under the Copyright Act, no part may be reproduced by any process without written permission. Inquiries should be made to the publisher.

Typeset, printed & bound by
Southwood Press Pty Limited
80-92 Chapel Street, Marrickville, NSW

For the publisher
Hale & Iremonger Pty Limited
PO Box 205, Alexandria 2015

National Library of Australia Cataloguing-in-publication entry
Dykes, Barbara
  Spelling Made Easy.
  ISBN 0 86806 622 2

  1. English language – Orthography and spelling –
  Juvenile literature. I. Thomas, Constance. II. Title.
421'.52

Contents

    Authors' Note   *1*
    The terms used in this book   *7*

Section 1   What you should know before you start

1   The basic ideas   *11*
    The origins of the alphabet   *11*
    Borrowings from other languages   *13*
    Basic requirements   *13*

2   The overall teaching plan   *15*
    English Base Words   *15*
    Middle English Words   *16*
    Words derived from Greek and Latin roots   *16*

3   The growth of the English language   *18*
    The Roman influence   *18*
    Christianity   *20*
    Danes and Vikings   *20*
    The Normans   *20*
    The Middle Ages and printing   *22*
    Exploration and discovery   *22*
    The Industrial Revolution   *23*
    Discovery and invention   *23*

4   The method of instruction   *25*
    General hints for successful learning   *25*
    Curved letters   *26*
    The phonograms   *26*
    Method for teaching phonograms   *27*
    Method for drilling phonograms   *27*
    Straight line letters   *27*

	From phonograms to words	28
	Word practice and use	29
	Consonant joining	30
	Ongoing learning	30
	Markings to help spelling and pronunciation	30
	Prove your spelling	31
	Teaching of rules	31

Section 2 English Base Words
5   How to handle the Base Words of the language   *35*
    The vowel sounds   *35*
    Consonants   *36*
    Reasons for writing more than one letter for one sound   *38*
    Special features of English Base Words   *38*
6   The 38 spelling units of English Base Words   *41*
7   Examples and exercises for English Base Words   *54*

Section 3 Middle English words, including Invasion words
8   The additional sounds of Middle English words   *73*
9   Spelling units 39-55   *76*
10 Awkward sounds and spellings: 'er', 'air' and 'ough'   *82*
11 Spelling units 56-58   *84*
12 Some foreign spellings   *86*
13 Spelling unit 59   *89*
14 Examples, dictation exercises, and homophones   *90*

Section 4 English words from Latin and Greek
15 How to understand words built from Latin and Greek   *99*
16 Spelling units 60-63   *103*
17 Prefixes and suffixes: examples and exercises   *105*

Section 5 Appendices
1   How the voice is produced   *115*
2   The difference between vowels and consonants   *116*
3   Writing tips   *117*
4   Breaking words into syllables   *119*
5   Spelling rules for English Base Words   *120*
6   Some extra help with spelling   *122*

A final word   *125*

Index   *128*

The terms used in this book

Definition of the terms used in this book:

Alphabet	A set of letters used to write a language.
Pictographic	Written with picture symbols.
Ideographic	Written with symbols representing ideas.
Consonant	A speech sound during the utterance of which the outgoing breath is impeded by bringing together two parts of the mouth.
Vowel	A voiced speech sound produced by air flowing from the lungs unimpeded. Each spoken syllable contains one vowel sound.
Syllable	A speech segment formed with one impulse of air from the lungs and containing one vowel or vowel phonogram, e.g. hot, hea ter.
English Base Words	Words derived from Old English (Anglo-Saxon) or from the speech patterns of this language.
Middle English Words	Words derived from the English of the middle centuries when attempts were being made to 'fix' various forms of words for writing and printing purposes.
Invasion Words	Words so-called by Mrs Elsie Smelt, being those which came into the English language from other European languages during the invasion of England by other

	European races, e.g. French from the Normans.
Suffix	A letter or syllable added to the end of a word in order to change its part of speech, i.e. the part that it plays in the sentence, e.g. enjoy, enjoy<u>ment</u>.
Prefix	A word element added to the beginning of a word in order to develop or add to its meaning, e.g. take, <u>mis</u>take.
Celts	A race of people who inhabited Britain before the Roman invasion.
Anglo-Saxons	Those people inhabiting Britain after the invasions by the Angles, Saxons and Jutes and before the Norman Conquest; they are also known as Old English.
Vikings	A fierce warlike people from Scandinavia who travelled the sea in long boats and raided and terrorised the people of Britain during the 8th to 10th centuries.
Danes	The Vikings and the Danes were all referred to as the Danes by the English and their raids were equally feared.
Normans	Inhabitants of Normandy who invaded and conquered England in 1066.
Phonograms	The written symbol(s) for a speech sound or unit, e.g. n, ck, ough.
Schwa	The indeterminate vowel sound representing the vowel in an unstressed syllable of spoken English, e.g. <u>a</u> lone, sys t<u>e</u>m, f<u>or</u> get.

BEFORE YOU START

Section 1

What you should know before you start

1. The basic ideas
2. The overall teaching plan
3. The growth of the English language
4. The method of instruction

1
The basic ideas

Be assured that everyone who can function adequately in today's world, can learn to speak and write good English and to read with confidence.

A teacher friend tells teachers,

'If a child can get himself to school he can be taught to read and write.

THE METHOD IS ALL IMPORTANT'

People wanting to improve their spelling must accept two things:
1. that English is an *alphabetic* language that is, it has a code with which to work out the printed word;
2. many English words have been derived from other languages.

1. The origins of the alphabet

1 *Early pictographic writing*

2 *Ideographic writing (modern Chinese)*

3 ἐν ὁ Θεὸς τὸν κόσμον, ὃν μονογενῆ, διὰ νὰ μὴ εἰς αὐτόν, ἀλλὰ νὰ ἔχῃ	4 A thing of beauty is a joy forever.

Alphabetic language *Alphabetic language*
(Greek) *(English)*

Early writing was pictographic — that is, pictures were drawn for words.

However, as life became more complex and people needed to express more ideas, the picture language proved inadequate. One cannot draw pictures of abstract ideas like courage, beauty, or dreams, so an ideographic writing system developed in which symbols stood for the words, both things and ideas. In this case the symbols mostly bore no relationship to the things which they represented.

About 2000 BC it was discovered that words consist of a series of separately uttered sounds. Moreover, a limited number of sounds was put together in different sequences. Therefore a written symbol was devised to represent each *speech sound*. This marvellous invention enabled people to write down any word they could say by recording the speech sounds in the correct sequence.

This provides us with a two-way operation. Once we know the symbols, we can work out the written word by translating each part into its correct speech sound.

The difficulty with our language arises because we have only 26 letters to represent the 44 basic sounds of English, so some letters must be used to 'say' more than one sound:

cycle   pancake

Furthermore, sometimes two letters and, in a few cases, three or four letters are used to say one sound:

fetch   rough

But the less common forms can be classified for easy learning. Association is a powerful aid to learning, so learning to handle all words of similar habits at the one time is vital to grasping English spelling.

2. Borrowings from other languages

The second thing we must appreciate is that English has taken words from many other languages over a long period. Events that shaped the history of the English people have had a strong influence on the development of the language, and we must know something of these events in order to understand the language.

The English language has been thousands of years in the making; today it is a world language spoken by more than 700 million people of many races. It is the language of diplomacy and of the United Nations; there is no manuscript of scientific, philosophic, cultural or religious importance in the history of man, which has not been translated into English.

Thus we might say that the whole of the history of Western Civilisation has played some role in making the English language.

Basic requirements

We have said that English is an alphabetic language.

In order to learn an alphabetic language there are certain requirements that are absolutely essential.

1. It must be understood that the words we speak are made up of only 44 different basic sounds. It will help if we know the formation of, and how to produce, all these single sounds individually. This is starting at the very beginning. (See Appendix 1, p. 115, for information about how the voice is produced.)
2. The student must be able to *hear* each of these single sounds in words and be able to join single sounds into words. For example, can you hear each sound in the following words?

thrift (5)	ring (3)	shrub (4)
script (6)	tempt (5)	splash (5)
scrap (5)	trudge (4)	clasps (6)

    Say them missing out any one of the sounds and experience the difference!
3. We must know the difference between the way vowels and consonants are spoken. (See Appendix 2, p. 116.)

4. In the early stages we must say each sound as we form each letter.

Correct formation of letters in writing helps to establish the firm association (connection) between the *sound* and the *symbol*.

5. We must understand what a syllable is. (See Appendix 4, page 119.)

These five points are very important. At least one of them will present some difficulty to everyone having trouble with English spelling. Any one of these points that is not fully grasped must be practised.

Maximum progress cannot be expected until all these fundamental points are thoroughly understood.

In a one-hour lesson, a five-minute segment at the beginning and at the end will usually be adequate to ensure a firm grasp of any aspect that is troublesome.

The 'schwa' sound

In the rhythm of everyday speech, any vowel in an unstressed syllable can be shortened to make the sound of a as at the beginning of alone. This is known as the 'schwa' sound and is written thus ə in dictionaries. It may occur in any part of the word, e.g. mother, cathedral, submit, derive, shorten, connect. It makes spelling from hearing more difficult, so it is important to emphasise vowel sounds for spelling and thereby develop an understanding of spelling patterns. By so doing, the speech of a student is also greatly enhanced.

An understanding of the schwa sound is particularly important in the study of words derived from Greek and Latin roots. (See section 4, pp. 97-112.)

2
The overall teaching plan

As Mrs Elsie Smelt, author of *Complete Guide to English Spelling* (Longman Cheshire, Melbourne, 1983) realised, by going through the dictionary word by word, English words can be classified into *three* distinct groups for easy learning:

1. Early English Base Words.
2. Invasion Words.
3. Words formed by adding prefixes and suffixes to a root derived from Latin or Greek.

For the purposes of this programme we have called the divisions:

1. English Base Words.
2. Middle English Words including Invasion Words.
3. Words formed from Latin and Greek roots.

1. English Base Words

These are simplified forms of Old English words, and are often words for basic needs and occupations. These words were simplified in the middle centuries (see Chapter 3).

Old English	became	*English Base Word*
runnan)	—	run
irnan)		
hyttan	—	hit
sunne	—	sun

When students learn how these words work, they will be able to spell all of them with confidence.

2. Middle English Words

These are Invasion Words and new, fixed forms of old words.

e.g. **tea** came into English through the French **thé**, which is pronounced half way between English long $\bar{e}$ and long $\bar{a}$.

The spelling of **boat** resulted from the way the word was pronounced in different dialects (**bat, bot**).

With the beginning of printing in the 15th century attempts were made to fix English spelling in order to reduce variations from region to region. Middle English Words comprise fewer than 14 per cent of the total number of English words. They are mainly the words in which the vowel sound is spelt with two letters (e.g. **ow, ea**).

3. Words derived from Greek and Latin roots

These are the sophisticated words of the language and are handled in a totally different way from the other two groups.

These words predominate in the vocabulary of educated, articulate adults. To be unfamiliar with the way they work is to limit one's language ability to that of a child.

Note the difference in level of sophistication:

a. Based on Early English only:
   The man and the woman were wed and went to live on the edge of the wood.

b. Including new English words:
   The gentleman galloped up the road on his new bay mount.

c. Including words from Latin and Greek:
   A nutritious diet must include a quantity of protein and plenty of vitamins and minerals.

The words of Latin or Greek origin are formed by adding a prefix or suffix to a root taken from Latin or Greek.

Example 1
tract comes from a Latin word meaning 'draw or drag'.

Prefix	Root	Suffix	Word	Meaning
	tract	or	tractor	that which draws or drags
ex (out of)	tract		extract	to draw out
dis (away)	tract		distract	to draw away from
re (back)	tract	ion (noun ending)	retraction	that which is drawn back

Example 2
dict comes from a Latin word meaning 'say or speak'.

Prefix	Root	Suffix	Word	Meaning
	dict	ion	diction	speech
pre (before)	dict		predict	to say in advance
pre	dict	able (able to)	predictable	able to be said in advance
un (not) + pre	dict	able	unpredictable	not able to be said in advance

The *prefix* changes the *meaning* of the word.
The *suffix* changes the *function* of the word in the sentence.

However, the human element enters into the making of language and it is not always as clear-cut as the foregoing examples suggest. But the ability to deduce meaning by analysing words in this way increases with practice.

So there you have the overall plan, and that is how we shall approach the study. We will learn how to handle the base words first, and go on, step by step, from there.

But first of all, let us look at the events that have contributed to the growth and development of the English language, and consider the far reaching effects they have had on its spelling.

3
The growth of the English language

The Base Words of the language are mostly derived from those used by people who inhabited England between the 5th and 9th centuries — the Anglo Saxons. The languages used in Britain before that time have survived only in the Celtic tongues of Gaelic and Welsh.

Many of these Base Words were very long like those of other early languages. They were shortened in the Middle Ages.

hloefidge	—	lady (the one who kneads the loaf)
hlaford	—	lord (the breadkeeper)
geenawan	—	know
wealcan	—	walk

The Roman influence (approx. 55 BC-400 AD)

When the Roman Empire became very powerful, its armies conquered much of North Africa, extending right around countries bordering the Mediterranean and across almost to the borders of India. The Romans finally conquered Britain in 55 BC.

During their occupation of over 400 years, the Romans changed Britain a great deal. They built many roads (some of which still exist), large houses around courtyards, and public baths with heated floors, brightly decorated rooms and a plentiful water supply. They built a wall across the country between England and Scotland (Hadrian's Wall) to keep out warring northern tribes, and parts of the wall still stand. They brought many civilising influences to those early inhabitants. When the Roman Empire became unmanageable and began to crumble, the Romans withdrew their armies from Britain; but they left behind a very strong influence on the culture of the Britons, including the alphabet and a knowledge of the Latin language. Thus began a long process of absorption into English of Latin words, of Greek via Latin, and of Latin via French. As Anglo-Saxons travelled through Europe, they learnt words from the Romans. Examples of Latin words absorbed into the English language during these early times are,

wall	castle	act	domestic
tower	tiles	scene	servant
line	educate	calendar	civilian
porch	punish	October	

After the Romans withdrew from Britain there was peace for a time but the warlike tribes from the north, the Scots (from Scotland) and the Picts (from northern England) continually raided the southern parts of Britain. Eventually the southerners sought help from the Angles and Saxons (from country roughly where Germany is today) and from the Jutes from Jutland. The Angles, Saxons and Jutes drove back the invading tribes from the north, but later they returned as raiders themselves. Some liked the green and fertile country so much that they stayed and settled in southern England.

The Roman buildings fell into ruin in these times because the newcomers did not understand town life. They were good farmers who knew how to clear trees and plough land, and warriors who loved fighting, feasting, bright clothes and jewellery.

It is said that of all the invaders, the Anglo-Saxons exercised the greatest influence on the early Britons and that Anglo-Saxon Celtic culture provided the basis of the people we today call the English. (Even the word *English* is derived from *Angles*.)

With the coming of the Anglo-Saxons there was comparative peace for the English people until about 700 AD. In this period new words and customs were absorbed, such as:

plough	lady	dye	ale	Alfred
hedge	lord	fight	song	Harold

Christianity

Christianity first came to Britain in Roman times but the Christians were pushed westwards by the heathen invaders. In 596, St Augustine landed in Kent (in south east England). Christianity then spread quickly and churches and monasteries were built. Often only monks could read and write, so they established schools in the monasteries. Education and religion were closely knit. Many more Latin words were brought into the language to explain religious and philosophic ideas:

testament	bible	pray	minister	salvation
script	chapter	matins	bless	benediction

Danes and Vikings

Between 700 and 900 AD the Vikings, a warlike people from Scandinavia, terrorised the peoples of Western Europe and the British Isles. They sailed in long, shallow-draft vessels, stealing noiselessly up the rivers at night and plundering the small settlements. All western European folk living along rivers (in France, Spain, Portugal, for example) feared the Vikings who would burn and plunder, seize produce and stock, capture women and children, and terrorise the small settlements. The attacks were sudden and people were taken unawares.

The Danes, who first came as robbers, later settled in the east and north of England where Danish communities sprang up. They proved to be good farmers.

The language of the Danes, Old Norse, was similar to Old English, being also of Germanic origin. But many of its words were much shorter than those of Old English and were soon absorbed into the language. From this time English began to drop its inflections, making the language much simpler than it had been.

sun	die	egg	sky	rag
tree	birth	steak	thing	skin
want	time	skirt	Thursday	Sunday

The Normans

The Saxon king, Alfred, spent many years fighting invading

Danes. When at last he defeated them, he forced them to become Christians. He rebuilt churches, brought scholars to England, and started schools. For several generations England became a united kingdom.

In 1066 William the Conqueror came across from Normandy (part of modern France) and defeated King Harold at the Battle of Hastings. He ruled his newly-acquired lands very firmly.

The Normans introduced many new ways of doing things in the areas of sport and pastimes as well as in the way people were governed. The feudal order of lords, barons, knights, soldiers, villeins (partly free peasants) and serfs (servants) was established. They also influenced architecture. Many fine castles and romanesque cathedrals were built and remain scattered throughout England to this day. Some words from this period are:

mutton	peasant	chivalry
beef	servant	gentry
port	castle	enclosure

So, from this time, there were three languages in use in England. The ruling classes, being Norman, spoke French; Latin remained the language of religion and learning; while both French and Latin were used for science and law. Although the conquerors tried to make French the official language of England, English was far too popular to be replaced. But from then on, even up to the present day, speaking French has carried social prestige.

Because of this intermingling of languages, modern English includes many synonyms — that is, words whose meaning is approximately the same — but each one has developed its own mood or shade of sophistication.

note / letter / missive / epistle
play / frolic / gambol / caper
sad / wretched / unhappy / despondent
ask / question / enquire / interrogate

Despite all efforts to the contrary, it was the speech of the ordinary people that remained dominant, enriched and invigorated by the influence of the invaders.

The Middle Ages and printing

The invention of printing machinery in the 15th century enabled more people to learn to read. Prior to this, writing was mostly done by monastery scribes; now clerks were required to prepare written matter for printing. An attempt was now made to 'fix' spellings. Until this time, there were wide variations in spelling and pronunciation in different regions, and there were many additions of invasion words whose pronunciations differed from those of English. This 'fixing' accounts for some of the seeming irregularities in English spelling.

Exploration and discovery

With printing came books, and knowledge began to spread. Explorers from European countries sailed farther and farther away from home. People no longer believed that the world was flat and that if they sailed far enough westward they would drop off the edge.

Christopher Columbus, a Spaniard, discovered America in 1492 and it was later settled by the British. Vasco da Gama found a route to India around the Cape of Good Hope (South Africa), thus opening up the East with its treasures of precious metals, food and spices.

The two most famous English explorers were Sir Francis Drake and Sir Walter Raleigh.

It is easy to see how the discovery of new lands, new customs and new foods brought new words to the language:

From South America:

        tobacco   potato

From American Indian:

        moccasin   tepee   kayak

After the discovery and settlement of Australia, some Aboriginal words became universal:

        billabong   galah   barramundi
        kangaroo   brolga   boomerang

The Industrial Revolution

In the 18th Century the Industrial Revolution took place in England and for the first time work or industry moved out of the home into factories, and systems of paid employment were established.

New words were adapted from other languages.

From Latin (via French)
- manufacture   hence   factory
- employ   hence   employment
- machine
- engine
- industry

Discovery and invention

Every discovery led to a need for new words. Every invention had to have a word to name it. Such inventions as electric power and motor cars added many new words to the language.

| spindle | pump | print | lever | petrol |
| pulley | valve | type | cogwheel | brake |

After the Industrial Revolution there came, over time, a revolution in communication.

morse code	transmitter	television (TV)
wireless	radio	satellite
soundwave	telephone	rocket

We coin new words to name new things. Often the new name describes what the invention does. Take **telecommunication** as an example

tele (from afar) + **communication** hence **Telecom**!

We also have words made from the initials of several words so that a simple word can express a complex idea.

QANTAS — Queensland and Northern Territory Airline Service.

LASER — Light Amplification (by) Stimulated Emission (of) Radiation.

So you can see that words have sprung into being because people needed to express something they were thinking or doing, things they were discovering or inventing.

When you are aware of these influences and see how they have affected the language, words will take on a new meaning and your understanding of the language will be much broader. Spelling will be much easier and more interesting as you see where all the words you are acquiring fit into the tapestry of our language.

"I guess I'm not letter-perfect."

4
The method of instruction

General hints for successful learning

1. Good posture ensures a free supply of oxygen to the brain and thereby helps it to function at its full capacity.
2. A left- or right-handed person should position the writing paper at the same angle as the forearm of the writing arm. The non-writing hand should steady the paper.
3. A six-sided pencil is helpful for showing the student the correct grip. The thumb and forefinger grasp the pencil just above the sharpened part and one flat side of the pencil should be partly visible in between. The student should be taught to hold the pencil correctly from the very beginning. (See Appendix 3, p. 117 for illustrations.) It is much better at first for children to use a soft pencil, say 2B, so that they can rub out mistakes and improve their work. This prevents the uncorrected error from becoming imprinted on the memory.
4. Lined paper should always be used and precise letter formation encouraged. Children like precision and generally respond to its demands. They learn to strive for a high standard in everything they do, even the smallest task.

Note. If children are colour blind, they may not see correctly some coloured lines in exercise books.

Instruction for *every student* begins with learning the sounds represented by the 26 single letter phonograms as shown on page 41-53.

Curved letters

Children learning to read and write for the first time are taught first the *eight curved letters*.

    a   c   d   f   g   o   q   s

In writing, these letters all begin with a curve which starts at the point of 1* on the round clock face, goes up towards 12 in a backward curve, on down through 10 and so on, without lifting the pencil unless a separate stroke has to be made, as with f.

The phonograms

The phonogram 'cards' on pp. 41-53, 76-81 and pp. 103, 104, represent all the common spelling units of English. In the bottom right-hand corner are symbols of the International Phonetic Alphabet. These are mainly for specialists.

It is a good idea for students to make their own phonogram cards using project board. They should be made larger than the illustrations — say approximately 12 × 10 cm, with the phonogram drawn up to 5 cm in height. Students can make their own spelling lists on the back and older students can write in rules or notes for their own reference.

The 'cards' are divided into three sections:

Phonograms used in
1. English Base Words
2. Middle English and Invasion Words
3. Words from Greek and Latin roots.

All the common sounds that the phonograms represent are mostly shown *in order of their frequency of use*.

e.g. **a** as in **cat** is the most common sound for this letter

The **aw** sound of **a** is the least used.

On the back of each card example words are given together with the rules governing the use of that phonogram.

---

* In Modern Cursive Script the curve starts at the point of 12 on the clock.

Method for teaching phonograms
The vital thing is the *saying* of the sounds *as* the phonogram is written.

A set of the phonogram cards is most helpful at this stage.
a. The students *see* the phonogram on the card as the teacher holds it up.
b. The students *hear* the sounds of the phonogram spoken clearly by the teacher.
c. The students *write* the phonogram themselves.
d. They *say* its sound/s *as they write it down*.
e. They *see* the phonogram *as* they write and speak its sound/s.

Thus students are using all the sensory channels into the brain at *the one time*.

Capital letters are taught only as they are required.

Method for drilling phonograms
It will be necessary to test students' knowledge of the phonograms and this is the way we have found successful.
1. *Test*
    a. Select a few of the phonograms already learnt.
    b. Dictate the sound(s) of the first phonogram to the students, who then write that phonogram from the sound/s you have given them, saying it to themselves as they write.
    c. Repeat the process with each card in turn.
2. *Check*
    d. Now show the correct card for the first phonogram dictated.
    e. The students then say the correct sound(s) for that card.
    f. They correct their own written phonogram.
    g. Repeat steps d-f with each card tested, in turn.

The teacher can then give practice with any that were wrong. A few minutes at the beginning and end of each lesson is usually sufficient.

Younger students often learn these phonograms more quickly than older people.

Straight line letters
See Appendix 3, pp. 117-118, for tips on handwriting skills.

When writing, all the letters except the eight curved letters begin with a straight line. (See Appendix, p. 117.)

Again the pencil should not leave the paper unless there is a separate part

The letters start at the top and go downwards except for two, e and z, which begin with a *horizontal* straight line going from left → to right.

e z

From phonograms to words

When students know thoroughly a number of single letter phonograms you can give them the chance to put two or three together, sounding the combination correctly. The joining of sounds needs practice. It is helpful to show students how to continue uttering the sound of the first phonogram until they say the second.

For this exercise, use the first sound of each phonogram.

ad	ac	ag	as
da	ca	ga	sa
od	oc	og	os
so	go	do	co
fac	gad	fas	saf
doc	gos	gof	sag

These do not need to be words because students are learning to *decode*, and also to think in *syllables*. (At this stage they should learn what a syllable is — see Appendix 4.) They are in fact learning *parts* of much longer words which they will later be able to break up into simple decoded syllables:

| ad | ad vise | dis ad van tage |
| se | sep ar ate | con sec utive |

You can then dictate such combinations for them to write down. This is particularly helpful for training the ear to *listen* and the brain to *transmit* what it hears to the hand that is writing.

The number of combinations increases with each new phonogram learnt, and at this stage the student is able to decode and recognise *real word* combinations:

Dad	cab	tap	gas
fog	sit	pal	pen
it	lip	nap	top

For some students, such words become sight words almost immediately. For others it will take much longer.

Students continue to learn new phonograms each day, at their own speed, until they know them all thoroughly.

Word practice and use

As the students learn to write each new word, it is a good idea to enter it into a spelling book. We have used a system of spelling markings. See pp. 30-31.

The learning of words follows the same general pattern as that for phonograms. However, first the teacher should say the word clearly and then use it in a sensible sentence so that its meaning can be readily understood.

> lid   Please keep the lid on the vegemite.

The teacher then sounds the word as they write it on the board (or lined paper).

At the same time the students write the word, sounding each part *as they write*. They then say the whole word as it is pronounced in normal speech.

They do not copy. When they have finished writing the word they can then look up and check it with that of the teacher on the board.

From the start, students should also practise using each word by making up their own oral sentences.

Soon they can try writing sentences of their own, sounding out each word as they write it. Each sentence should be checked and corrected by the teacher or parent.

Consonant joining

Sounding two or more consonants together may need more practice than sounding a consonant plus vowel, as in the earlier exercises.

These can be practised in groups:

cl	clam	clot	clip	club
cr	crab	crop	crib	crawl
st	stem	stab	stop	stuff
	test	fast	cost	crust
str	strip	strap	string	strong

Ongoing learning

Continue adding new phonograms till all are learnt.

Introduce various sound combinations as they arise and enlarge the vocabulary using a spelling list.

Test the spelling of words so that each student continues to learn at his/her own speed. There is nothing frightening about testing when it is part of the normal learning routine.

Practise well, both orally and in writing, each new thing that the student learns.

Punctuation. Teach this as you go. Introduce capital letters *and their usage* as they are required; full stops will be learnt with the writing of the first complete sentence.

N.B. There is no harm in introducing a phonogram out of order should it arise. For example, **ph** may be encountered in the word **elephant** before the teacher has arrived at the third section of this book. Students will learn that this is a phonogram of Greek origin when they reach this section.

Markings to help spelling and pronunciation

These markings can be made when a word is first entered into a vocabulary (spelling) book or in exercises.

a. To emphasise that a vowel is short the dictionary mark may be used above it: căt, păck.
b. Long vowels are marked as in the dictionary with a long stroke above: thēme, hōtel.

c. When silent e makes a previous vowel long, we can link the final e to its vowel thus: nāme, lāthe.
d. Phonograms of two or more letters should be underlined so that they can be recognised as a unit: bri<u>ck</u>, bri<u>dge</u>.
e. Words can be separated into syllables: stā tus or stā/tus.
f. Silent letters can be marked with a small zero sign above: house°, climb°.

Prove your spelling

Some students enjoy proving that the English language is in fact mostly regular. This method of marking spellings can be used to 'prove' the spelling of words. The process helps to impress the various features of the language on the mind. In such exercises it is a good idea to write words in syllables until it has become a habit to think in syllables:

<u>per</u> man ent

Teaching of rules

These should be taught *as they arise* and reinforced frequently. Children assimilate spelling rules through using them as they go along. It is necessary, however, to be sure that they do understand them. Migrants, on the other hand, need to have them explained.

Example A
Use the following procedure when teaching the rules for spelling English Base words.

As soon as the students are competent in (1) sounding three letter words, e.g. **hop** (consonant, vowel, consonant) and (2) understanding the difference between *short* and *long vowel* sounds, *then* they can be taught the use of the *silent finale* **e** to make a previous vowel long, (see p. 36) e.g. **hop** becomes **hope**.

An older student can write the rules into an exercise book. They should be revised regularly.

Charts may be made for the younger reader and hung on the wall for reference.

Example B
Once students (1) understand what a syllable is and (2) have been introduced to two syllable words, when they meet a word such as **ta ken or ho tel** *then* they can be taught the rule that **a e o** and **u** are usually long (say their own name) at the end of a syllable. (See page 64.)

This rule helps with reading, and its significance is apparent when dealing with the rules for doubling. (See page 39.)

Example C
The first time that a child writes a sentence which is a question, either alone or with the teacher, *then* he/she should be taught the use of the question mark and shown how to write it.

In this way punctuation becomes an integral part of language instruction.

Ideally, grammar should be taught in the same way, thereby generating an understanding of language structure and a respect for its 'mechanics'.

Section 2
English Base Words

5. How to handle the Base Words of the language

6. The 38 spelling units of English Base Words

7. Examples and exercises for English Base Words

5
How to handle the Base Words of the language

The word *phonogram* means a 'spelling unit' — **phono** meaning **sound**, **gram** meaning **written**. It literally means 'the writing of a sound'.

There are 38 phonograms used in the words referred to in this chapter classified as *English Base Words*.

Vowels

        a e i o u

Note: y can also be a vowel. See p. 66.

The vowel sounds

There are only five short and five long vowels in English Base Words. It is important to be able to recognise the difference between short and long vowel sounds.

   ᵕ above the vowel denotes a short sound.

Say ă ĕ ĭ ŏ ŭ in (sharp) staccato fashion:

        ă — as in **hat**
        ĕ — as in **bed**
        ĭ — as in **pin**
        ŏ — as in **lot**
        ŭ — as in **mud**

— above the vowel denotes a long sound.

Now say the five long sounds. They are the same as the names of the letters.

$$\bar{a}\quad \bar{e}\quad \bar{i}\quad \bar{o}\quad \bar{u}$$

It is vital to understand that in these *early English* words each vowel can say two sounds — short and long.

	Short	*Long*
Letter a can say	ă as in hat	ā as in hate
e can say	ĕ as in pet	ē as in Pete
i can say	ĭ as in pin	ī as in pine
o can say	ŏ as in not	ō as in note
u can say	ŭ as in us	ū as in use

Notice how the addition of the silent letter e in the second column makes the previous vowel say its own name. It tells the reader to say the vowel that way.

So when we see the letter a in these *Base Words* we know it most often says ă (short); *but* if we see it followed by a single consonant plus another vowel, it will usually have the long sound.

e.g.   hŏt   but   hōtel
        tăp   but   tāper
        dĭn   but   dīning

Consonants

Now let us look at the *consonant* sounds of the *English Base Words*.

There are 21 *single letter consonants* which each say only one sound in English Base Words:

How to handle the Base Words of the language 37

b c d f g h j k l m n p q(u)* r s t v w x† y z

There are ten two-letter and two three-letter consonants which mainly say one sound.

th wh ng wr kn sh ch ck tch
dge ed or

At first underline these phonograms when writing them to impress on the mind that these, two (or three) letters say only one sound.

The student will then see the combination as a single unit, that is, as a phonogram.

<u>wr</u>ap   fet<u>ch</u>

Now, having learnt the
ten vowel sounds
twenty-one single consonants
ten 2-letter consonants
two 3-letter consonants

you can write the *thousands* of phonetically spelt Base Words of the language. (For a list of words for practice and testing, see p. 69.)

Start with the words that use only single letter phonograms.

First, read them. Moving from left to right, we make a distinct sound for each letter in turn

1 2 3
p a t

Then, write them. We listen for the single sounds of the spoken word and we write *one letter* for *each sound*.

Remember, we are not relying on sight to remember these words. We are using our minds to *apply what we know* of the working of the alphabet and the *code*.

---

* Strictly speaking, q is an invasion letter from French and is pronounced k (as in cheque). The u represents the w sound in English. However, we have left this phonogram in the Base English section because of its conventional place in the alphabet. Similarly, x is an invasion letter of Greek origin.

† is actually a combination of two sounds, k and s.

Reasons for writing more than one letter for one sound

Having established the practice of writing one letter for one sound, we can now learn the reasons for writing more than one letter for one sound. So far we know of only two categories of spelling where a second letter is necessary;

1. In a long vowel pattern — to make the previous vowel say its own name.

    m a̲ k e̲   t i̲ m e̲

2. In two-and three-letter consonant combinations such as **ng**, **dge**,

    si**ng**   ba**dge**

At this stage, if the student can correctly spell up to 90 per cent of the words in a dictation test he/she is ready to cope with a few special features of Early English Words — the times when we add an extra letter for reasons that are different from those already mentioned.

Special features of English Base Words

1. After the five short vowels ă ĕ ĭ ŏ ŭ in short one-syllable words, we often double **f**, **l**, **s**, **z**

    puff   will   mess   buzz

There are a few other cases, like **odd**, **add**, **egg**.

2. Using **tch**, **dge** and **ck** (instead of **ch**, **j**, **k**)

A. **tch**
After the five short vowels ă ĕ ĭ ŏ ŭ we spell the ch sound **tch**.

    la**tch**   di**tch**

There are five exceptions to this rule:

    much   such   rich   which   sandwich

B. **dge**
After the five short vowels, ă ĕ ĭ ŏ ŭ we spell the j sound **dge**.

    ba**dge**   e**dge**

How to handle the Base Words of the language

C. ck
After the five short vowels ă ĕ ĭ ŏ ŭ we spell the k sound ck.

clock   luck

Note. This does not apply if another consonant follows, e.g. act. See Latin and Greek (blue) section p. 101.

	tch	dge	ck
ă	catch	badge	pack
ĕ	fetch	hedge	deck
ĭ	stitch	midge	sick
ŏ	notch	lodge	frock
ŭ	hutch	fudge	truck

3. There is one other occasion when we add an extra letter.

When we add an ending beginning with a vowel, such as

ed,   est,   er,   ing

to a one-syllable word with a short vowel between two consonants like

hŏp   hŏt   bĭt

we double the last consonant before adding the ending.

hop	hopped	hopping
hot	hotter	hottest
bit	bitter	bitten

Thus, when we *hear* a word spoken with a *short* vowel in the first syllable, we know we must double the consonant that follows when spelling that word.

clutter	Mummy
kitten	supper
dinner	ladder

Conversely, when we hear a word spoken with a *long* vowel in the first syllable, we know that we do *not* double the following consonant:

bāker	sūper
ūsing	lātest
tāped	slōping

40 *Spelling Made Easy*

There are very few exceptions to the foregoing. One is that the letter v is never doubled.

quiver

Another is that the ŭ sound before v is often spelt with an o

love   glove

N.B. English words do not end with v.
English words never end with i or u. (You is the one exception.)

The student will now know how to handle practically all the Base Words of the language.

For a summary of the rules to observe in spelling English Base Words refer to Appendix 5, page 120.

THE FAMILY CIRCUS By Bil Keane

"Why do I have to keep writin' in these K's when they don't make any noise anyway?"

6
The 38 spelling units of English Base Words

a 1	1 **a**
a **A** æ eɪ ɑː	The letter **a** has three common sounds: ă ā ar (short) (long) (usually before 2 consonants) an *cake bath at make path am came pass cat late last flat tape task bran state father * **e** makes the previous vowel long (say its own name) **a** can also say **aw** (for **aw** see card 50) e.g. after **w** — **warm water** with **l** — **tall chalk falter** etc.
b 2	2 **b**
b **B** b	The letter **b** can say only one sound bat cab It is sometimes silent bin rub rubber comb debt bed crib rubbing lamb doubt bun club dumb blunt bulb climb Doubling Rule: We double **b** only when it follows a short vowel ă, ĕ, ĭ, ŏ, ŭ, and we are adding an ending beginning with a vowel. **r u bb i ng**.

3

c

C

C   k s

---

3   c

The most common sound of this phonogram is **k**;

Base English	Middle/Invasion English
k	**s**
followed by	when followed by
a, o, or u	**e, i, or y**

cat	cent	city	cycle
cut	cell	circle	cyclone
cap	centre	cinders	cygnet
crust	celebrate	cinema	cylinder

4

d

D   d

---

4   d

The letter **d** can say only **d**

dog	nod	dip	hidden*
dig	lid	dot	Daddy
drop	dent	trod	ladder
dusk	dark	grid	muddiest

* Doubling rule:
We double **d**, only when it follows a short vowel and we are adding an ending beginning with a vowel — (see card 2)
(vowel + 2 consonants + vowel)
e.g. **nodding ladder**

5

e

E   ε i

---

5   e

The letter **e** has two sounds

ĕ (short)		ē (long)
pet	pen	she
bed	men	he
leg	end	me
hem	help	we
		*the

In **Pete, these** etc., the final **e** makes the previous vowel long (say its own name)

*e In this word says **ē** (long) only before vowels
e.g. **thē apple**

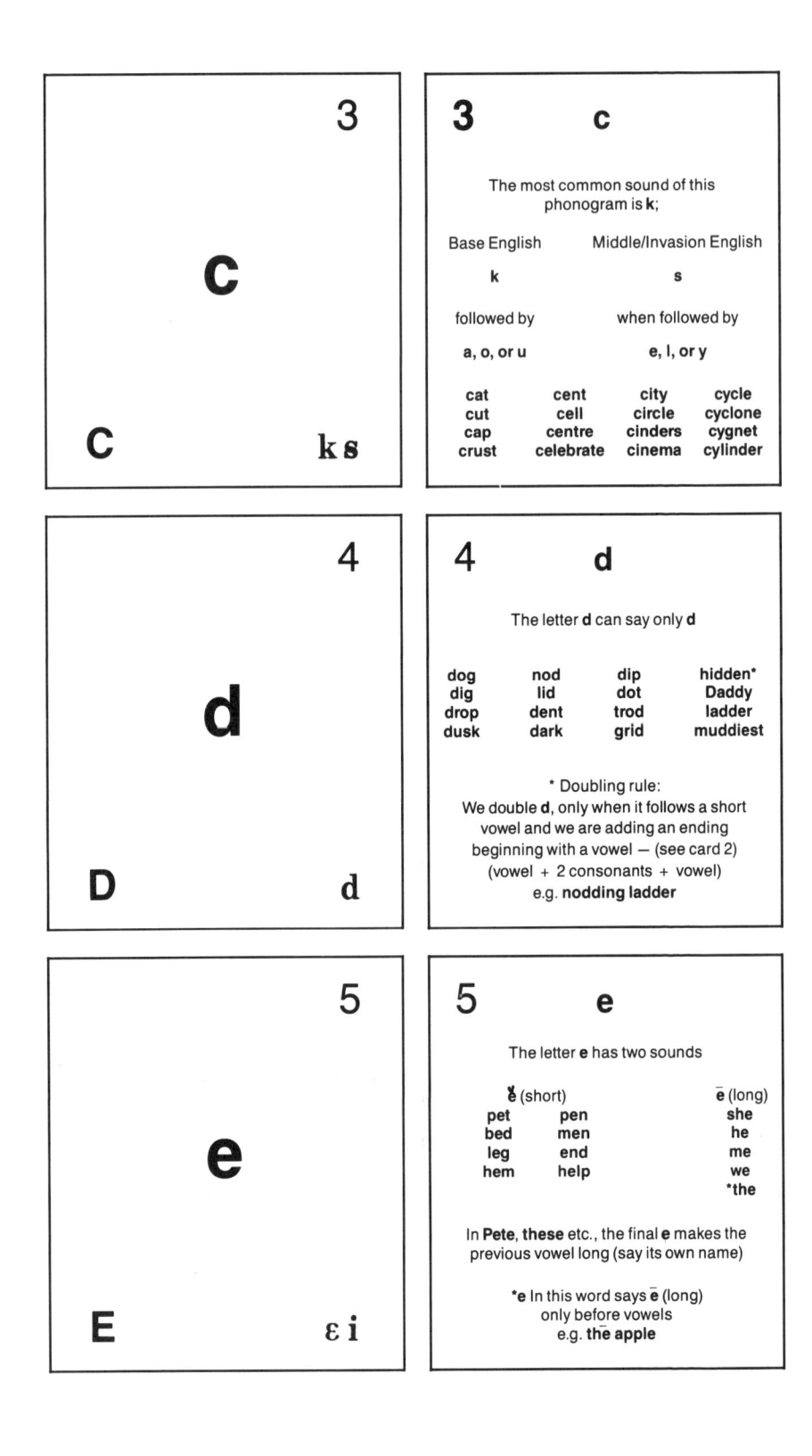

6

f

F   f

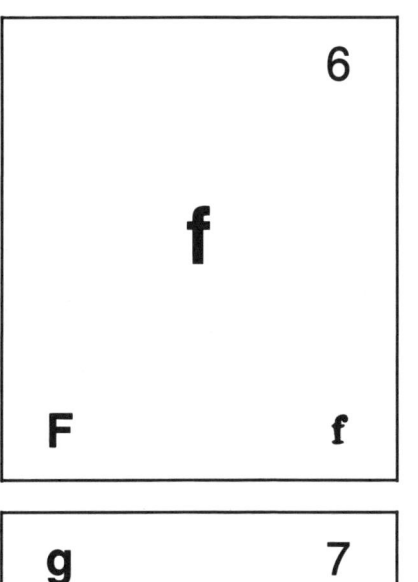

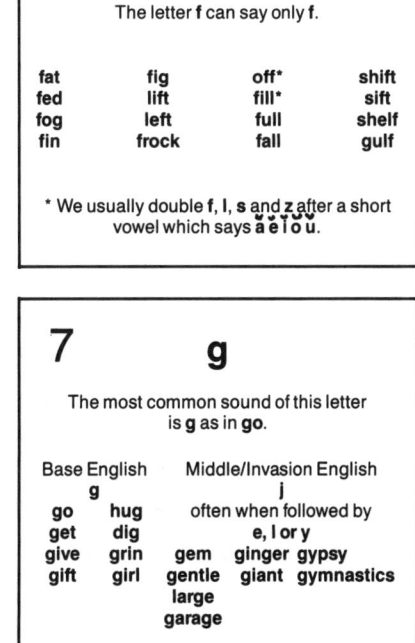

6   f

NOTE Always write the cross stroke from left to right.

The letter **f** can say only **f**.

fat	fig	off*	shift
fed	lift	fill*	sift
fog	left	full	shelf
fin	frock	fall	gulf

* We usually double **f**, **l**, **s** and **z** after a short vowel which says **ă ĕ ĭ ŏ ŭ**.

7

g

G   g dʒ

---

7   g

The most common sound of this letter is **g** as in **go**.

Base English   Middle/Invasion English
    g   j

often when followed by
e, i or y

go	hug			
get	dig			
give	grin	gem	ginger	gypsy
gift	girl	gentle	giant	gymnastics
		large		
		garage		

*logging
begging

* Doubling rule, see card 2

8

h

H   h

---

8   h

Unless preceded by **c, t, p, s** or **w** to form phonograms (**ch, th, ph, sh or wh**) this letter always says **h**, with breath.

          h

hat	hill*
hem	hunt
hid	hold
hurry	perhaps

The letter **h** is used only at the beginning of a syllable.

*for **ll**, see card 6

9

i

I   ɪ aɪ

---

9   i

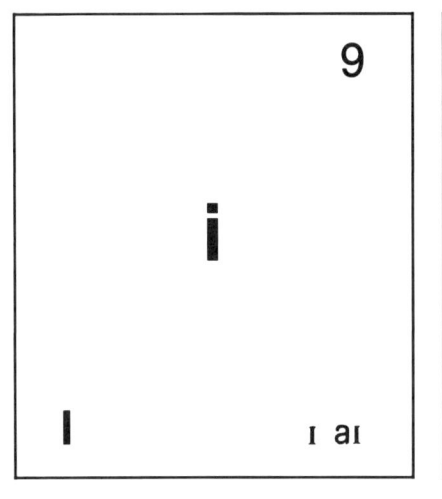

The letter **i** starts with a straight line and the dot is put on afterwards.
It can say two sounds

	ĭ short		ī long	
is	fit	trim	hike*	blind**
in	rip	drip	bite	pride
if	bin	spit	time	glide
it	sit	flint	side	grime

* **e** makes the previous vowel long
(say its name)
i can say **ee** if it follows French spelling
e.g. **machine, routine, police, Pauline.**
** **i** often has the long sound before
2 consonants e.g. **kind, blind**

10

j

J   dʒ

---

10   j

The letter **j** always says **j**.

jam	jet	joke
jog	job	jelly
jug	Jill*	jump
jig	Jack	adjust

j is used only at the beginning of a syllable
and never at the end of a word.

If we hear the **j** sound after a short vowel
which says **ă, ĕ, ĭ, ŏ, ŭ**, it is always spelt **dge**
(see card 35).

* See rule on doubling **f, l** and **s**, card 6

11

k

K   k

---

11   k

The letter says only **k**. It can be called **tall k**
or 'Kay' (its name).

keg	kill	*pink
kit	milk	thank
Kim	kiln	bunk

* Note how the **n** becomes **ng** (card 28)
before **k**.

The **k** sound after short vowels **ă, ĕ, ĭ, ŏ, ŭ**,
is always spelt **ck** (see card 34).

An exceptional word — **kleptomania**,
from Greek

12

l

L   l

---

12   l

The letter **l** can say only **l**

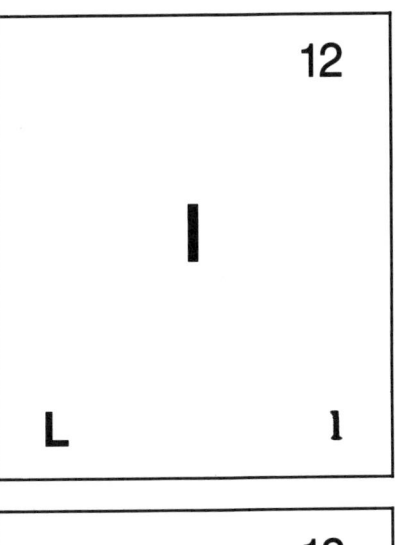

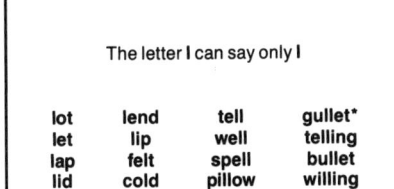

lot	lend	tell	gullet*
let	lip	well	telling
lap	felt	spell	bullet
lid	cold	pillow	willing

We often double **l** after the short vowels
ă, ĕ, ĭ, ŏ, ŭ.

l is sometimes silent e.g. **palm, talk, walk**.

* For rule on doubling see card 2

13

m

M   m

---

13   m

The letter **m** can say only **m**

mop	hem	trim	**Mummy***
man	him	mend	drumming
mud	dim	dump	hammer

* For rule on doubling see card 2

14

n

N   n

---

14   n

The letter **n** can say only **n**

not	fun	bent	dinner*
net	din	blunt	winning
nap	pan	lent	thinnest

See also cards 31 and 53 **kn** and **gn**;
both these say **n**, the **k** and **g** being silent.

* For rule on doubling see card 2

15

o

O

o ɒoʌu

15   o

The letter **o** can say three main sounds.

ŏ (short)	(lōng *)	ŭ	also o͞o
top	hope	come	
lot	tone	mother	do
sob	note	front	to
knob	home	done	who

Note: learn the last column by saying and writing the words several times.
O often has the long sound, **ō** before two consonants e.g. **cold won't**.
* In these words, final **e** makes the previous vowel long, (say its name).

16

p

P   p

16   p

The letter **p** can say only **p**

pin	cup	help	trapper*
pet	tip	plan	tapping
pod	lap	stop	stoppage

* For rule on doubling, see card 2

p

17

qu

Q   kw

17   qu

The letter **q** is a curved letter; **u** is a straight line letter, but **q is** always followed by **u** so we put them together as a unit.

qu says **kw**

quick   squash*
quite   squat
quack   squander

* Note: see special rule about the **ŏ** sound after **qu**, **w** and **wh** on card 23

QANTAS is a combination of the first letter of six words; Queensland And Northern Territory Aerial Services.

18 r

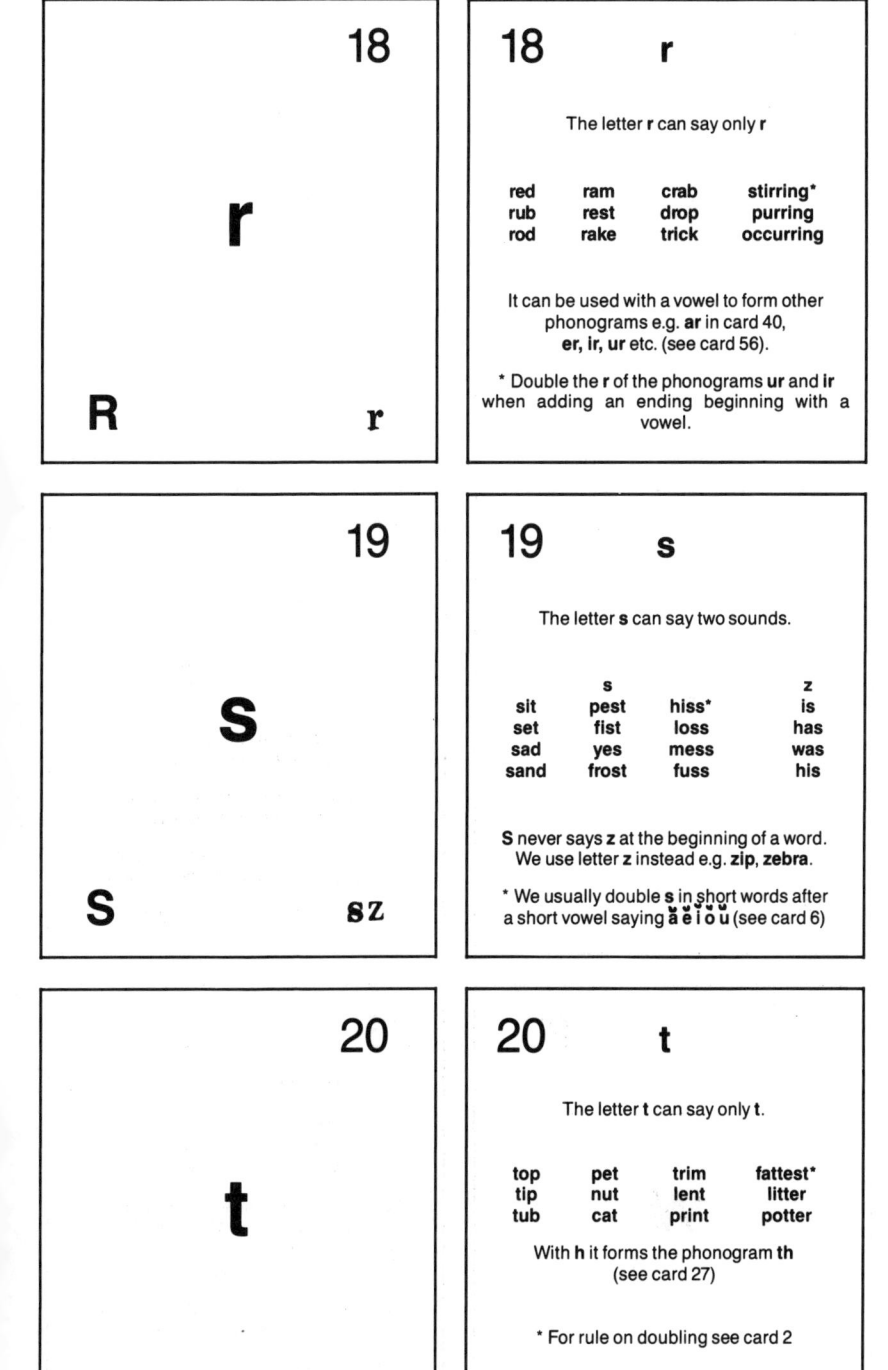

r

R r

---

18 r

The letter **r** can say only **r**

red	ram	crab	stirring*
rub	rest	drop	purring
rod	rake	trick	occurring

It can be used with a vowel to form other phonograms e.g. **ar** in card 40, **er, ir, ur** etc. (see card 56).

* Double the **r** of the phonograms **ur** and **ir** when adding an ending beginning with a vowel.

---

19 s

S

S sz

---

19 s

The letter **s** can say two sounds.

		s	z
sit	pest	hiss*	is
set	fist	loss	has
sad	yes	mess	was
sand	frost	fuss	his

S never says **z** at the beginning of a word. We use letter **z** instead e.g. **zip, zebra**.

* We usually double **s** in short words after a short vowel saying ă ĕ ĭ ŏ ŭ (see card 6)

---

20 t

t

T t

---

20 t

The letter **t** can say only **t**.

top	pet	trim	fattest*
tip	nut	lent	litter
tub	cat	print	potter

With **h** it forms the phonogram **th** (see card 27)

* For rule on doubling see card 2

21

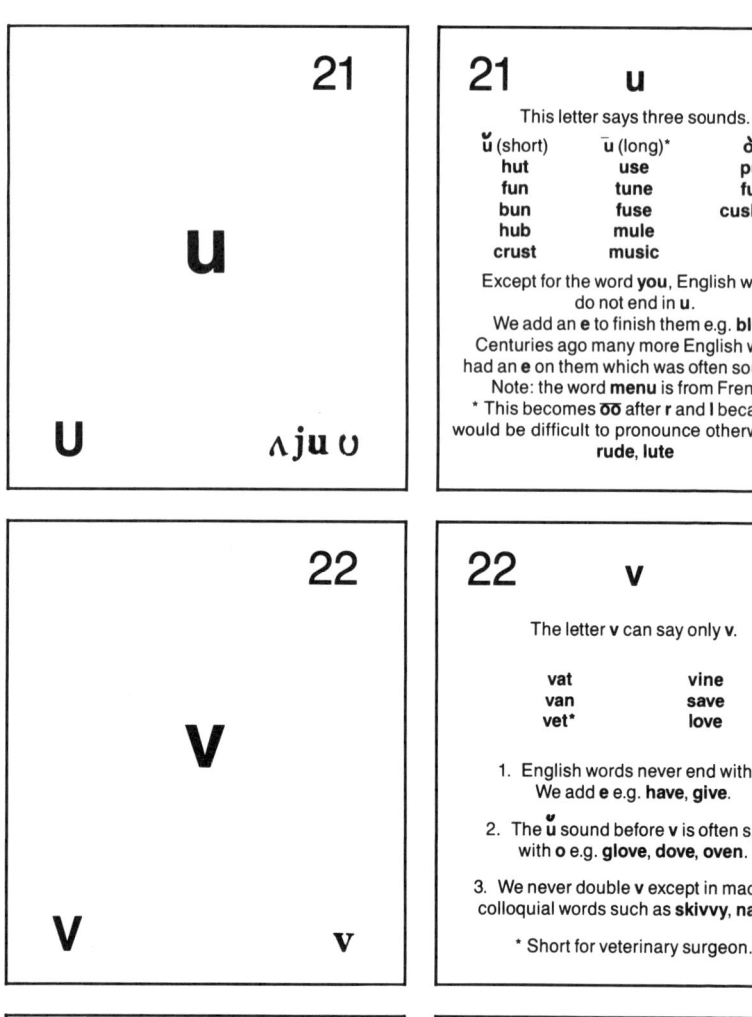

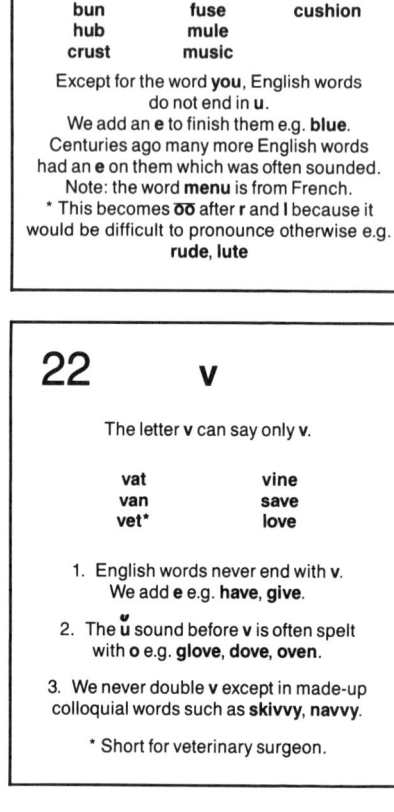

u

U   ʌ ju ʊ

---

21 u

This letter says three sounds.

ŭ (short)	ū (long)*	ŏŏ
hut	use	put
fun	tune	full
bun	fuse	cushion
hub	mule	
crust	music	

Except for the word **you**, English words do not end in **u**.
We add an **e** to finish them e.g. **blue**.
Centuries ago many more English words had an **e** on them which was often sounded.
Note: the word **menu** is from French.
* This becomes ōō after **r** and **l** because it would be difficult to pronounce otherwise e.g. **rude, lute**

22

V   v

---

22 v

The letter **v** can say only **v**.

vat	vine
van	save
vet*	love

1. English words never end with **v**. We add **e** e.g. **have, give**.

2. The ŭ sound before **v** is often spelt with **o** e.g. **glove, dove, oven**.

3. We never double **v** except in made-up colloquial words such as **skivvy, navvy**.

* Short for veterinary surgeon.

23

W   w

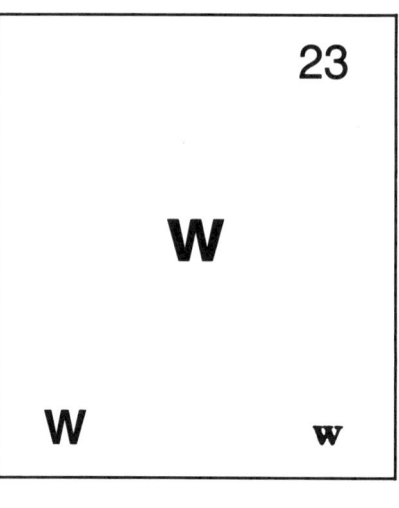

23 w

The letter **w** says only **w**.

wet	west
win	will
wag	wipe

Watch for **ow**, **aw** and **ew** at the end of a syllable, (see cards 49, 50 and 51).
These are vowel phonograms and the **w** is not sounded.

With **h** and **r** it forms the phonograms **wh** and **wr** (see cards 30 and 32).

Special Note: The ŏ sound after **w**, **wh** or **qu** is often spelt with an **a**, e.g. **was, wasp, what** and **quarrel**.

24 x

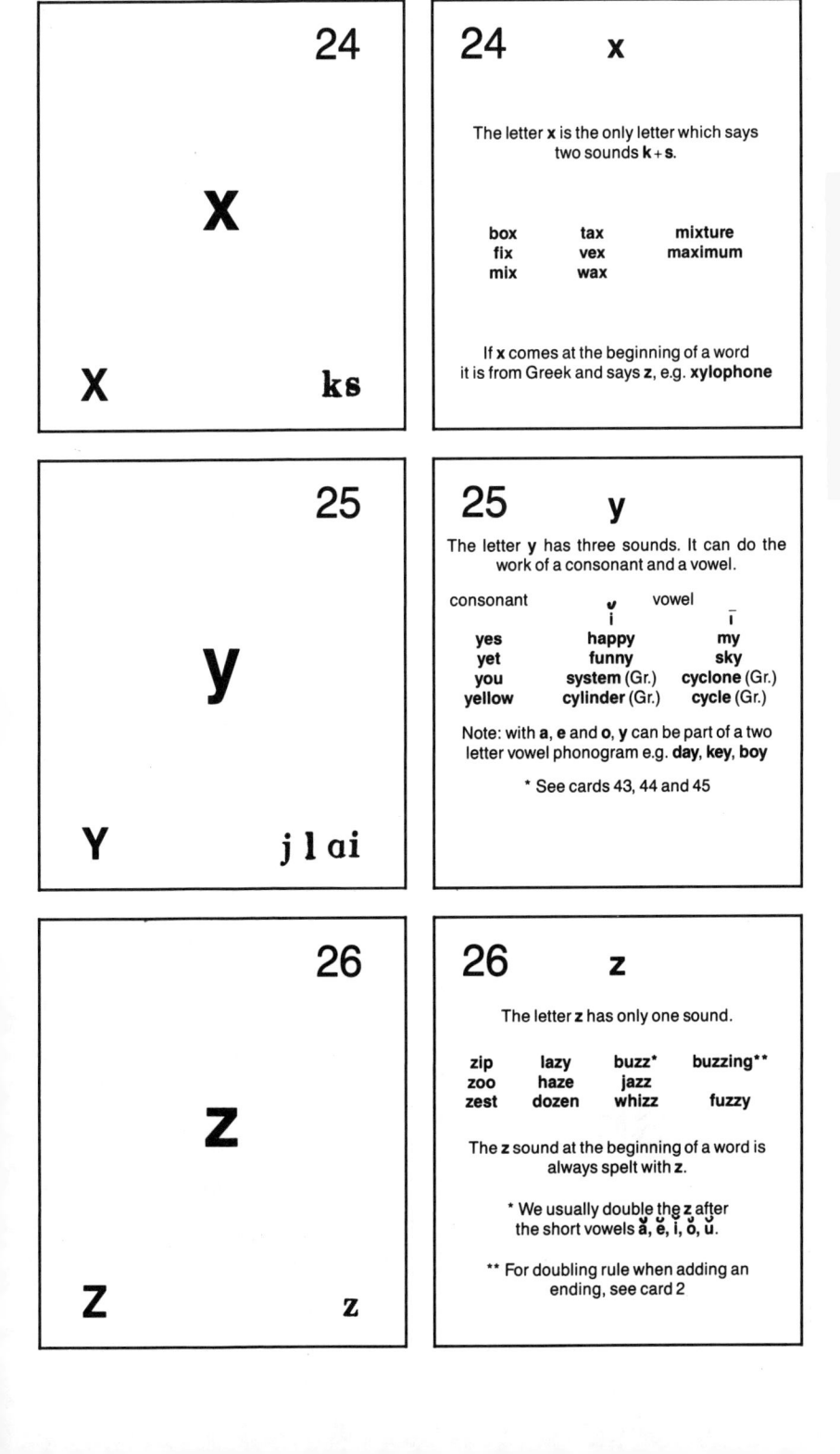

The letter **x** is the only letter which says two sounds **k** + **s**.

box	tax	mixture
fix	vex	maximum
mix	wax	

If **x** comes at the beginning of a word it is from Greek and says **z**, e.g. **xylophone**

---

25 y

The letter **y** has three sounds. It can do the work of a consonant and a vowel.

consonant	ĭ (vowel)	ī (vowel)
yes	happy	my
yet	funny	sky
you	system (Gr.)	cyclone (Gr.)
yellow	cylinder (Gr.)	cycle (Gr.)

Note: with **a**, **e** and **o**, **y** can be part of a two letter vowel phonogram e.g. **day, key, boy**

* See cards 43, 44 and 45

---

26 z

The letter **z** has only one sound.

zip	lazy	buzz*	buzzing**
zoo	haze	jazz	
zest	dozen	whizz	fuzzy

The **z** sound at the beginning of a word is always spelt with **z**.

* We usually double the **z** after the short vowels **ă, ĕ, ĭ, ŏ, ŭ**.

** For doubling rule when adding an ending, see card 2

27

th

θ ð

---

27   th

The phonogram **th** has two sounds

th	th
The sound of **th** is soft in **thin** (an unvoiced sound).	The sound of **th** is hard in **that** (a voiced sound).
thin	that
thing	them
thong	this
throb	these
bath	mother
myth	lathe

28

ng

ŋ

---

28   ng

This phonogram can say only **ng**. (Close the back of the throat to say this sound.)

bang	hang	length	finger*
sing	rung	wring	longer
long	bring	strong	

The **ng** sound occurs only after a short vowel sound which says **ă, ĕ, ĭ, ŏ, ŭ**.

When **n** comes before **k** we say **ng** e.g. **think drank**.

* **g** is sometimes sounded when we add an ending beginning with a vowel.

29

sh

ʃ

---

29   sh

The phonogram says only one sound and is used at the beginning of a word:

ship   **shop**   **shot**   **shelf**

or at the end of a syllable. (For meaning of syllable see Appendix 4, p. 119.)

fish   **cash**   **dashing**   **washer**

It is not used at the beginning of a syllable after the first one — for this we use **ti, si or ci**, (see card 60).

station   **social**

30 wh

wh

hw

---

30 wh

We say this phonogram as **hw** (using more breath).
Although this sound is standard English, the **h** part of the sound is often dropped to become **w** only.
However it is very helpful in spelling to emphasise the standard pronunciation.

when	which
where	whip
why	whisper
what	whet

In the following words the **w** is silent
who, whom, whose, whole.

---

31 kn

kn

n

---

31 kn

This two-letter **n** is used only at the beginning of a base word.
(**k** is silent)

knit	know
knob	knapsack
knife	unknown
knot	acknowledge

---

32 wr

wr

r

---

32 wr

The two-letter phonogram **wr** says only **r**.
The **w** is silent

wrap	wring	written
write	wriggle	wrapped
wrist	writing	wrestle

wr is used only at the beginning of a base word
wrap **unwrap**

33 ch

ch

tʃ k ʃ

---

33 ch

The two-letter phonogram **ch** can say three different sounds, according to the origin of the word.

ch (Base English)	k (Greek)	sh (French)
chat	school	machine
chop	chemist	chef
chips	chaos	champagne
choke	charisma	quiche
*much	echo	chassis
*such	anchor	parachute
*rich	character	
*which		
*sandwich		

* These five are exceptions to **tch** rule. See card 36

34

ck

k

---

34 ck

This two letter phonogram we call two-letter **k**.

It is used only after a short vowel which says **ă, ĕ, ĭ, ŏ, ŭ.***

pack	neck	jacket
peck	knock	locker
lick	truck	bucket

* If another consonant follows the **k** sound, this rule does not apply
act, fact, acme, diction.

Note: **trek** is from Dutch
Yak is from Tibetan

35

dge

dʒ

---

35 dge

The three letter phonogram **dge** is used only after a short vowel
ă, ĕ, ĭ, ŏ, ŭ.

badge	fudge	badger	fridge*
edge	hedge	gadget	
dodge	midge	fidget	

Notice how the above words would appear without the **d**; hence we need the **d** to show that the preceding vowel is short.

* **fridge** is an abbreviation of refrigerator. The **dge** is needed to show that the vowel is short.

36   tch

Three letter phonogram **tch** is used only after a short vowel **a, e, i, o. u**.

catch	stitch	ratchet
fetch	scotch	kitchen
witch	clutch	satchel

There are five common exceptions **much, such, rich, which, sandwich** — also **lecher**

Sandwich was coined last century after the Earl of Sandwich who would order meat put between slices of bread, to save time. However the Romans before him did eat this way too.

37   ed

This is the two letter phonogram for the past tense ending of regular verbs

It says three things according to the previous vowel:

ed	d	t
	after **d** and **t**	
graded	loved	hiked
rotted	halved	hitched
folded	timed	packed
loaded	rubbed	fetched

38   or

This phonogram is also a little word on its own. Most people sound the **r** slightly. The Scottish sound the **r** strongly. Australians tend not to pronounce it at all.

for	lord	hornet	borer*
cord	sort	corny	storing
torn	port	storm	

* The **r** is fully sounded when adding an ending beginning with a vowel.

Note: Also **floor, door, poor** etc. (In standard English **poor moor**)

For other spellings of this sound see card 52.

7
Examples and exercises for English Base Words

The following pages, 54 to 69, contain lists for reading and dictation practice.

Single letter phonograms

N.B. It is a good idea to read lists both across and down.

1. The eight curved letters. Write and say the sounds of **a, c, d, f, g, o, qu, s**
   (a) singly;
   (b) in combination, using only short vowel sounds and first sound of **c,(k)** as in **cat**:

ad	ac	ag	as	od	oc	og	os
da	ca	ga	sa	so	go	do	co
	ac	qua	od	so			
	ad	ga	oc	go			
	af	da	of	fo			
	as	fa	og	quo			
	gac	sad	gof	cod			
	saf	caf	gog	dag			
	fad	dad	sog	fag			
	quag	gag	dog	quag			
		Dad	God				

2. Straight line letters
   (a) **b, h, i, j** — (using only first sound of **g(get)**).
   J is used only at the beginning of a syllable.

had	jib	fig	gas	job
gab	hid	gig	fob	jib

Examples and exercises for English Base Words   55

jab	sid	did	hab	hog
has	jif	his	quid	jog

a can now be learnt as a sight word and simple sentences read and written.

> Dad has a big dog.
> His dog had a jab.

(b) k, l, m, n

lad	Jim	lob	fan	nod
mad	sin	ham	fin	mod
dam	kid	him	on	lid
man	bid	kin	log	jam

The can now be learnt as a sight word.

> Jim hid the lid of the jam.

N.B. Children should make up oral sentences themselves, with all new words and write at least one or two a day.

(c) p, r, t, u

rub	pun	bun	pat	bat
cut	fun	cub	rot	tug
mud	tub	sun	dig	rap
run	rut	bit	rug	rot

> Pam sat on a rug in the sun.
> Rob dug in the mud.

(d) v, w, x, y — (diagonal)

van	wig	box	wet
bix	pox	vim	six
yam	wag	van	win
fix	wax	tax	yap

> Don has not got a top.
> Tim has six in a red box.

(e) e, z — (horizontal)

yes	sex	yum	zed
ten	mix	web	his
zip	zag	wed	Liz

> Has Ted got a zip in his togs?
> Yes, and a zig zag on the top.

3. More practice

   (a) Practice with ă.

jam	lad	gas	tab
had	ham	gap	bag
sad	vat	cat	lap
wag	pad	pal	pax
tap	fat	map	fan

   (b) Practice with ŏ.

Tom	dot	hog	sob
rot	top	box	cot
don	lot	hop	lop
not	fog	pod	dob
cod	hot	on	lob

   (c) Practice with ĕ.

pen	led	net	ten
leg	red	wet	hem
wed	fed	peg	let
den	Ben	pet	yes
bed	men	Ted	vet

   (d) Practice with ĭ.

tin	bit	hip	bin
fix	wig	sip	fit
win	tip	pin	dim
lid	mid	hit	lip
mix	his	fib	sin

   (e) Practice with ŭ.

tub	Mum	hub	sun
bun	rub	jut	hug
cub	but	bud	run
fun	hum	dug	sum
nut	gun	hut	rug

   (f) Practice with all short vowels.

hub	ten	set	dug
wax	rag	leg	cut
log	wit	hat	rim
vim	vex	sit	tag
not	yap	bob	got

Examples and exercises for English Base Words

Two and three letter phonograms

1. th has 2 sounds

(*soft*)	(*hard [voiced]*)	(for later revision)
thin	the	thump
thud	that	cloth
Beth	this	thing
moth	then	thank
thug	them	thong

2. wh

when	why
whip	where
whim	which
whiz	white
*what	whale

   *After w or wh the short o sound is often written with an a.

   N.B. In the following words the w is silent, (a relic from earlier times): who, whom, whose, whole.

3. ng

bang	wing	strong
ring	rung	bring
long	tang	sting
hang	sing	string
sang	rang	cling

4. wr — 2 letter r — the w is silent.

wrap	write
wrong	wrote
wring	wreck
writ	wrist
wren	wretch

5. kn — 2 letter n used at the beginning of a word. The k is silent.

knob	knee
knot	knock

knife	knack
knit	knuckle
*knoll	knickerbockers

* l, f, s and z are usually doubled at the end of words of one syllable. See p. 38.

6. sh — used at the beginning of a word and end of a syllable. For syllables see Appendix 4.

ship	cash	brush
shut	fish	crash
shall	wish	flesh
shed	dish	wash
shop	hush	shelter
		shabby

7. ch. This 2 letter phonogram has 3 sounds. In early English it was pronounced as in chair. For other sounds, see pp. 90-91.

chop	chest	cheese
chap	lunch	cherry
chum	chat	choose
chip	pinch	chocolate
chill	munch	chimpanzee

8. (a)
ck, tch, dge

ck and three letter combinations tch and dge are used only after a short single vowel.

back	deck	stack
sack	sock	stuck
luck	lick	crack
wick	pick	brick
tick	lock	truck

(b)
tch

batch	crutch
witch	stitch
fetch	wretch
hutch	stretch
match	scotch

Examples and exercises for English Base Words 59

N.B. Learn separately exceptions: rich, much, such, which, sandwich.

(c)
dge

edge	cadge	*fridge
badge	bridge	hedge
wedge	dodge	lodge
fudge	bludge	sludge
ledge	sledge	trudge

*Made up word from frig, an abbreviated form of refrigerator.

(d)
ck, tch and dge are used at the end of words of one syllable, but are sometimes followed by an unstressed syllable such as er, et, y, le, en.

pocket	bucket	docker	knocker
jacket	wicket	fidget	chicken
lucky	stocky	tickle	gadget
sticky	plucky	kitchen	ledger
ticket	stretcher	matchet	bludger

9. ed — past tense ending.
 (a) Sounded ed (after t or d) as in hated.

lift ed	load ed	blas ted	di vi ded
fit ted	wast ed	tempt ed	in vent ed
bat ted	list ed	trad ed	im port ed
part ed	hunt ed	bolt ed	cas tra ted

 (b) Sounded d as in loved.

loved	fared	im proved
tied	seemed	in jured
robbed	played	col oured
lived	carved	both ered

 N.B. Columns 1 and 2 are one syllable only.

 (c) Sounded t as in packed.

looked	baked	wrecked	knocked
liked	licked	stacked	blocked
picked	packed	spiked	flicked
joked	hooked	smacked	plucked

 N.B. These words are of one syllable only.

10. or

or	born	gorge	dor mant
ford	store	torch	for tune
sort	porch	storm	im port ant

Long vowel sounds

1. Silent final e makes the previous vowel long. A long vowel says its own name. See p. 36.

mate	made	late	brave
lane	lake	cave	skate
same	tale	wake	grape
tape	lame	cane	stale
name	wave	bake	shape

2. Although the same rule applies there are very few words in which e makes the previous e long. Usually we use other spellings such as ee and ea.

Pete	*theme
here	*scheme
these	*scene
	*concrete
	*complete

*Not early English words.

N.B. here, there and where should be sight words by now.

3.

line	side	mile	drive
time	like	hide	alive
pine	ride	dive	shine
hike	bite	fine	smile
mine	pipe	ripe	stripe

4.

pole	hope	pope	stole
hole	note	sole	stove
tone	home	hose	stroke
nose	poke	dope	broke
rope	bone	vote	drove

5. As with e there are a limited number of words in which u is lengthened by the following e.

tube	cube
huge	fuse
tune	nude
rude	mule
use	June

6. Final silent e can lengthen the previous vowel without a consonant in between.

tie	toe	due
die	doe	hue
lie	hoe	blue
hie	roe	true
fie	woe	clue

N.B. English words cannot end with i or u.

Consonant combinations and qu

1. i and o often have their long sound before two consonants and a its third sound.

mild	fold	fast	palm	calm
kind	pint	task	path	father
bolt	colt	glass	half	master
most	grind	calf	grass	plaster

2. Some practice lists for consonant combination.

   (a)
block	broke	clothes	crust
bluff	brace	clamp	crime
blade	broth	close	crash

   (b)
drop	dress	flesh	frog
drape	drudge	flock	frisk
drill	drift	fling	fresh

   (c)
glad	grim	hint	just
globe	grunt	haste	jilt
glaze	gruff	hump	jest

(d)	mist	plant	pram	rust
	mend	plot	prick	ramp
	most	pledge	prize	rink
(e)	slap	scrum	sprint	strip
	slate	scratch	sprang	stride
	slim	scrape	sprog	stroke
(f)	trust	whisk	yell	drum
	track	wrist	yank	brim
	trump	weld	blank	grope

3.
quit	quench	quick	queer
quell	quest	quid	question
quake	queen	quote	quiet

Plurals

1. Words ending with a consonant add **s** for plural.

cats	belts	desks	stumps
vans	plums	socks	cramps
pills	crisps	plugs	strips

2. Words with long vowel and silent final **e** add **s**.

homes	miles	saves	tribes
tapes	whines	tunes	slides
pines	bones	poles	plumes

3. Words ending in the sound of **s, x, z, ch** and **sh** add a syllable **es**.

dresses	buzzes	boxes	dishes
losses	fuzzes	fixes	witches
kisses	fizzes	taxes	lunches

4. Irregular plurals

(a) men   (b) sheep   (c) f to v loaves
     children   dice   knives
     oxen   fish   hooves

chicken	teeth	wives
women	feet	calves

5. **ie for y.** For interchange of **i** and **y**, see p. 67.

ladies	jellies	copies	minties
lorries	ponies	daddies	candies
berries	billies	cherries	pasties

c or k

1. The **k** sound is written **c** before **a, o,** or **u**.

cut	cost	cast
cat	cave	cold
come	cute	cuff
cud	cadge	cube

2. The **k** sound is written **k** before **e** and **i**.

kin	kettle	kick
kite	keel	kitchen
kilo	keep	kennel
kill	keg	kindy

N.B. There are many words now accepted as English but which are invasion words from other languages and therefore do not follow English rules, such as **kangaroo, kapok**. See p. 87.

3. The **k** sound before **t** is always spelt **c** (**act**). See p. 101.

Doubling f, l, s, and z at the end of one syllable words, after a short vowel.

After a short vowel.

1.

hill	still	puff	miss
well	shall	tiff	less
cull	spell	gaff	buzz
bell	troll	whiff	whizz

(**bus** is an exception, being the shortened form of the Latin word **omnibus**)

2. l and s are also doubled after the third and fourth sounds of a and the third sound of u.

    grass   call   pull
    pass   ball   full
    glass   fall   bull

Doubling consonants. See p. 39.

1. When adding an ending beginning with a vowel.

hotter	stopper	hottest	winner
bitter	muddy	reddish	tapping
supper	letter	bunny	bitten
happen	written	chipping	chopper

N.B. Rule for 2 syllable words see p. 111.

2. Silent final **e** dropped —
Thus a single consonant indicates that the previous vowel is long.

dining	hoping	saved	baked
super	timer	wavy	diving
liking	chiming	maker	glider
making	widen	shining	bravery

Words of two or more syllables

1. a, e, o and u are usually long at the end of a syllable.

ba by	fi nal	wa ges	le ver
la bel	ha ted	to ken	
si lent	be gan	ta ble	wa ken
tu lip	na vy	du ty	

2. One syllable is stressed (emphasised) more than the rest in any word — it is usually the word root.

'hap py	'pup py	mo 'tel	ad 'mit
'ta ble	'bas ket	re 'lax	re 'ply
'but ter	'mat tress	in 'vent	in 'vade
'kit ten	'hop ing	su 'perb	re 'gret

Examples and exercises for English Base Words

3. More words with more than one syllable.

   N.B. Words are usually separated between 2 consonants but phonograms are *not* split.

   (a) Two syllables

ne ver	plen ty	traf fic	be have
plan et	gos pel	hope less	trum pet
hund red	ze bra	mag net	gra vy
ham mer	rab bit	hamp ster	peb ble

   (b) More than two syllables — N.B. These words do not belong to the early English section.

bal con y	dif fi cult	re spon si ble	ca ra van
e nor mous	po ta to	dis in fec tant	tel e scope
fan tas tic	bar be cue	in ter es ting	ra di o
hor ri ble	tres pass er	ther mom e ter	lem on ade
com pan y	re mem ber	or din ary	croc o dile

Extra vowel sounds and two sounds of s

1. Third sound for a as in path. See also p. 75.

fast	cask	bas ket
path	past	fath er
ask	grass	plast er
bath	mask	nas ty

2. The fourth sound for a as in all. See also p. 75.
   (After w and before l)

all	walk	al ways
call	talk	al to geth er
tall	wa ter	wal nut
wall	al so	wal rus

3. a sounded as short ŏ after **qu**, **w** and **wh**.

was	wash	wal let	qua rrel	swap
want	wasp	wad dle	qua lity	swat
what	wad	wan der	quan ti ty	squash
watch	wrath	twad dle	quan da ry	squab ble

(exception — wob ble)

4. Third sound of **o** as in **to**.

to	in to	move
do	on to	prove
who	un do	ca noe
lose	do ing	shoe

5. Fourth sound of **o** (ŭ).

come	none	does	co ver
son	done	moth er	ov en
front	won	hon ey	a mong
some	love	mon ey	an oth er

6. Third sound of **u** (o͝o).

put	bull	cush ion	pul let
full	pull	butch er	pul pit
bush	pus sy	pud ding	bul lock
push	su gar	bul let	bul ly

7. **y** as a vowel

Short ĭ as in baby		Long ī as in my	
la dy	en vy	my	dry
lor ry	tum my	by	fry
man y	emp ty	sky	why
li ly	jol ly	fly	im ply
hap py	cra zy	cry	de ny

8. The interchange of i and y.
   In English **i** is never used at the end of a word.

   (a) We avoid **y** in the middle of a word.

ti di ness	said	tas ti ness	mud di er
hap pi ly	paid	am pli fied	dir ti ly
bur ied	du ti ful	cudd li est	mag ni fied
sil li er	co pi er	hun gri ly	qua li fi ca tion

   (b) This is not normally done when it would split a vowel phonogram, or cause an unnatural vowel sequence.

grey er	joy ful	em ploy er	be tray ed
ly ing	dy ing	de lay ing	car ry ing
pay ment	pray ing	con vey or	hur ry ing

Sounds of s and silent letters.

S has two sounds.

1. (a) soft as in sit.

soft (voiceless)		hard (voiced)	
Single s	*Double s*	*Hard*	*Before e*
sit	pass	has	wise
bus	toss	was	hose
soft	miss	his	use
fast	lass	hers	fuse

   N.B. Hard **s** is never used at the beginning of a word — only **z** e.g. zip.

   (b) Soft s after k, p and t   Hard s after other letters

present tense	*plurals*	*present tense*	*plurals*
works	desks	falls	times
jumps	socks	lives	waves
takes	pots	hums	prizes
hopes	wasps	sends	travels

2. Silent letters.

b	t	others	
comb	of ten	mus cle	hon est
lamb	fas ten	ghost	build
doubt	has ten	receipt	John
thumb	whis tle	au tumn	Thom as

3. Silent **e** used to give second syllable its vowel. See p. 122, item 4.

    le follows double consonant, except m and n.

lit tle	ax le	can dle	buck le	lev el
mid dle	hand le	min gle	tem ple	tin sel
puz zle	ank le	gen tle	tan gle	tun nel
peb ble	jun gle	un cle	sta ble	la bel

4. (a) No job e — the e which once served a purpose but no longer does. See p. 122, item 5.

are	else	loose	false
none	mouse	nurse	horse
house	vase	grease	please

   (b) Silent **e** also follows **v** at the end of a word. See p. 122.

love	live	have	sleeve
move	give	prove	leave
live	dove	glove	believe

1. **Compound words** — the joining of two whole words, one qualifying the meaning of the other thus forming a third.

no one	tea set	ice berg	under wear
some time	else where	where ever	news paper
sun set	dough nut	for ever	grid iron

2. Prefixes and suffixes from words ending in two **l**s, e.g. full, drop one **l**.

al so	force ful	un til	beau ti ful
ful fil	harm ful	al ways	sor row ful
wel fare	wel come	help ful	ful fil ment

English Base Words for dictation

Use these for dictation tests for phonograms on pp. 41-53. These words are unlikely to have been learned 'by sight'. So students will have to work them out from their own knowledge of the way these words work.

pad	bit	den	fame
rid	cad	gift	hug
jet	for	limp	map
not	tripe	quip	ride
stem	strip	sop	torn
vat	whine	fetch	bike
miss	knife	thin	thud
then	shot	hush	chimp
such	whip	tube	rang
nude	trod	brunt	slate
fact	tempt	shove	stuck
graded	packed	liked	loved
dill	gull	tiff	dress
bridge	stitch	buzz	thong
clam	snatch	chilly	clap
shift	thrive	nip	brag
stunt	pledge	gripe	graft
cramp	spite	lists	sprang
glum	chipping	wrist	bone
squid	badge	lots	blink
lost	struck	frizz	trust

A special note:

1. The **schwa** sound —
   The **schwa** sound is the short indeterminate 'a' sound, being the common pronunciation of any vowel phonogram in an unstressed syllable e.g. 'a' in 'a drink' and 'alone'.

a̱ go	a̱ mong	moth eṟ	fas te̱n
a̱ lone	fo̱r get	fath eṟ	a̱n oth eṟ

Section 3

Middle English words, including Invasion words

8. The additional sounds of Middle English words

9. Spelling units 39-55

10. Awkward sounds and spellings: 'er', 'air' and 'ough'

11. Spelling units 56-58

12. Some foreign spellings

13. Spelling unit 59

14. Examples, dictation exercises and homophones

8
The additional sounds of Middle English words

These are the phonograms described in this chapter, classified as Middle English words, with some useful aids for memorising them. These are the phonograms on pp. 76-81.

ee	ar	oa	ie
ai/ay	oi/oy	ei/ey	oo
ea	igh	ou/ow	au/aw
ew	or	gn	gu/gh/ui
eigh			

(For the awkward sounds and spellings of **er**, **air**, **ough**, see pp. 82, 83.)

In this section we will learn how to spell words fixed for printing and words that have come into English from other languages.

Many of these are words in which the vowel sound is spelt with two or more letters,

        ow   ee   ai   etc

They comprise only a very small percentage of the words in the language and can be learned more easily if presented in groups.

They are taught in the same way as described in chapters 4 and 5 and the rules should be memorised.

Some of the phonograms in this section can 'say' more than one sound; for example, **ea** has three sounds

eat   bre$\overset{2}{a}$d   ste$\overset{3}{a}$k
meat and bread are great

In addition, some of the vowels and consonants already learnt can take on an extra sound or sounds.

A. *Consonants*
1. The phonogram c which *always* says k in English Base words, has a second sound s.
    Whenever c comes before e, i or y we know it will have s sound.

    cent   city   cycle

2. Phonogram g which has only soft, unvoiced g sound in English Base Words *may* say j if followed by e, i or y

    gem   ginger   gym

    (j sound came from French and was a new sound in English.)

    If the g before e, i or y *is* pronounced as j, then you know that the word must be an invasion word, probably from French.

    large,   frigid,   gentle

3. Phonogram y which says y as in yet is a consonant in English Base Words.
    Now it has two more uses and can be used as a vowel.

    It can say i as in gym
    and ī as in sky

    N.B. English words never end with i, so if we need ĭ or ī sound at the end of a word we use y instead.

    baby   carry   lovely
    my   cry   deny

    Likewise i can be used instead of y in the middle of a word, so each has its job and each helps the other.

    tidiness

The additional sounds of Middle English words

4. Phonogram s may say z in many common words, such as

    is   has   was

and in plurals,

    things   boys   girls

It is never used at the beginning of a word — we use z instead.

    zip   zebra

5. Phonogram ch, as well as saying ch as in child can say k as in s_chool (from Greek)
and sh as in chef (from French)

B. Vowels

The letters e and i retain just the original two sounds, short and long.

1. Phonogram a, as well as saying ă$^{(1)}$ (tap) and ā$^{(2)}$ (tape) may also say

a³ (ah)	a⁴ (aw)
path	ball
task	water

2. Phonogram o, as well as saying ŏ$^{(1)}$ (not) and ō$^{(2)}$ (note) may also say

o³ (u)	ŏ⁴ (o͞o)
com_e	do
mother	to

3. Phonogram u as well as saying ŭ$^{(1)}$ (cut) and ū$^{(2)}$ (cute) may also say

    u³ (ŏo)
    put
    full

N.B. After l, r and s, the ū becomes o͞o as in lupin, rude, super because it is easier to say.

These are the only additions to the sounds of the phonograms already learnt in English Base words.

9
Spelling units 39-55

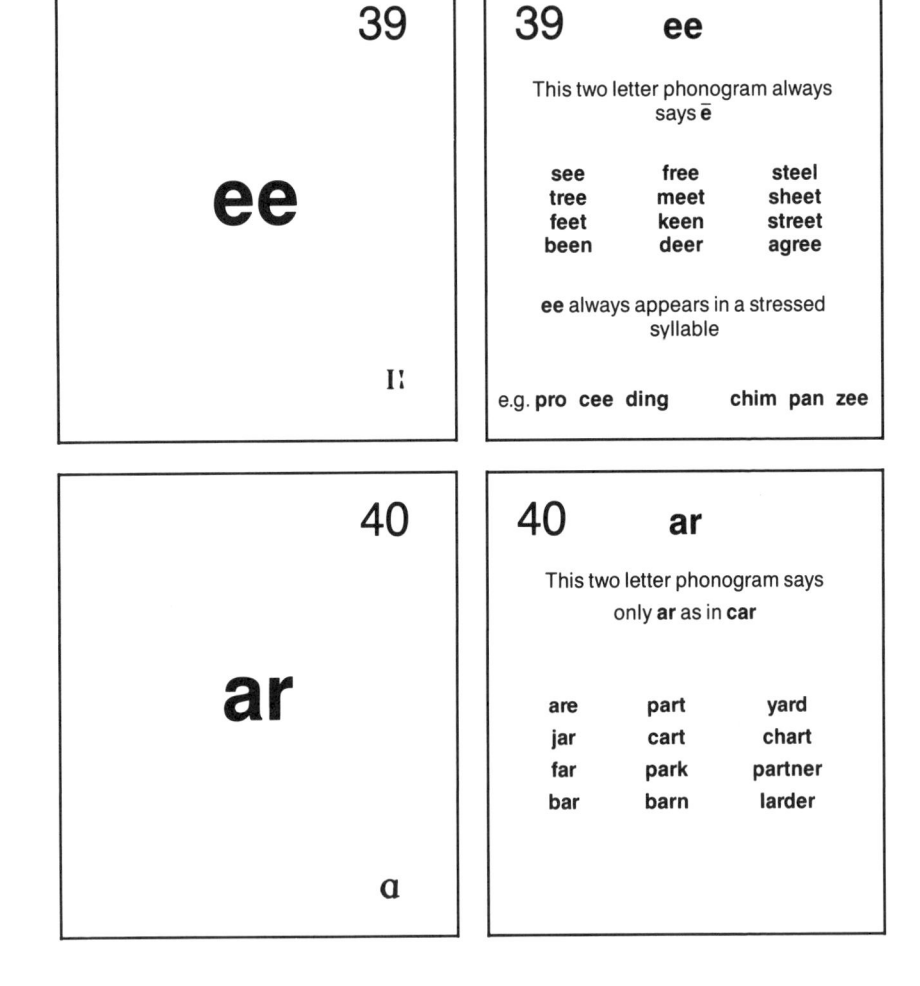

39

ee

ī:

---

39 ee

This two letter phonogram always says ē

see	free	steel
tree	meet	sheet
feet	keen	street
been	deer	agree

ee always appears in a stressed syllable

e.g. **pro cee ding**   **chim pan zee**

40

ar

a

---

40 ar

This two letter phonogram says only **ar** as in **car**

are	part	yard
jar	cart	chart
far	park	partner
bar	barn	larder

41

oa

oʊ

---

41   oa

This two letter phonogram always says only ō as in **goat**.

boat	load
coat	groan
road	float
toad	cockroach

42

ie

aɪ   i

---

42   ie

This phonogram has two sounds

ī			ē
pie	relied	piece	belief
lie	replied	grief	relief
tie	died	thief	achieve
die	cried	niece	handkerchief

See card 45 for when we use **ei**.

43

ai/ay

eɪ

---

43   ai/ay

The two letter phonogram **ai** and **ay** always say ā.
ai is never used at the end of a word.

ai		ay*	
rain	brain	say	play
main	train	day	stray
tail	strain	pay	display
fail	again	may	portray

* **ay** may appear in the middle of a word, either followed by a suffix, e.g. **payment**, or in a compound, **payday**.

44 oi/oy

oi/oy

ɔɪ

---

44 oi/oy

The two letter phonograms **oi** and **oy** always say **oy** as in **boy**.
oi is never used at the end of a word.

	oi		oy*
oil	coin	boy	ploy
coil	join	toy	destroy
soil	joint	joy	convoy
boil	loiter	Roy	annoy

* **oy** may appear
in the middle of a word
either followed by a suffix — **enjoyment**
or in a compound — **toyshop**.

---

45 ei/ey

ei/ey

i/eɪ

---

45 ei/ey

The two letter phonograms **ei** and **ey** have mainly two sounds:
ei is never used at the end of a word.

ei		ey	
ē	ā*	ē	ā
receive	vein	key	they
deceive	reins	monkey	grey
ceiling	reign	valley	prey
receipt		trolley	survey

* The old rule should say
'**i** before **e** except after **c**
and except when it does not say **ē**',
e.g. **vein, heifer, either, leisure, foreign**
exception: **seize**.

---

46 oo

oo

uʊ

---

46 oo

This two letter phonogram has two sounds, long and short.

ōo (long)		ŏo (short)	
school	moon	good	foot
pool	spoon	book	wood
too	broom	look	stood
boot	balloon	took	shook

Note: Also **oor** as in **floor, door** etc.

47

ea

iː ɛ eɪ

---

47   ea

This phonogram can be pronounced three ways

as in **m¹eat** on **br²ead** is **gr³eat**.

ē	ĕ	ā
tea	head	great
meat	bread	break
meal	deaf	steak
team	breath	
steam	tread	
dream	weather	
please		

48

igh

aɪ

---

48   igh

This three-letter phonogram says ī, we call it 'three letter i'.

high	sigh
light	sight
night	bright
tight	fright
fight	knight

49

ou/ow

au, u, ʌ, oʊ

---

49   ou/ow

ou mainly says three sounds.
Never use at the end of a word*

ou as in **loud**	ʊʊ	ŭ	also in a small group
found	you	young	soul
round	group	touch	shoulder
cloud	soup	double	poultry
proud	youth	cousin	boulder
mouth	tour	country	poultice

ow has two sounds

as in **cow**   ō
now, how, allow,   low, tow, show,
town, brown   throw

* Exception **you** can be learned as a sight word

50

au/aw

ɔ ɒ

---

50   au/aw

The phonograms **au** and **aw** mostly say one sound as in **Paul**, but **au** can also say ŏ.

au	ŏ	aw
as in **Paul**. Never used at the end of a word.		
cause	Australia	paw
pause	sausage	claw
haunt	cauliflower	draw*
taught	caustic	trawler
audience		

* When adding an ending beginning with a vowel we must take care not to introduce an **r** sound.
i.e. **draw ing**, not droring.

51

ew

u ju

---

51   ew

This two letter phonogram can say two sounds.

o͞o	ū
crew	few
blew	dew
flew	new
drew	stew
curlew	knew

For **eu** see card 62

52

or
Four spellings of **or**

ɔə(r)

---

52   Four spellings of **or**

or   which can be a little word on its own —
nor, cord etc. — see Card 38.

oar   to paddle with, **soar** etc.

oor   as in **floor** and **door** — see Card 38.

our   as in **your, pour, four**, etc.

53

gn

n

---

53   gn

This phonogram is the two-letter **n** that may be used at the beginning or the end of a word.

gnome	sign
gnaw	feign
gnash	reign
gnat	resign
gnarl	consign

kn, also saying **n**, cannot be used at the end of a word

See card 31.

54

gu
gh
ui

g g u

---

54   gu gh ui

These unusual spellings come from different sources.

*gu	*gh	ui from French
guest	ghost	fruit
guilt	ghastly	juice
guess	aghast	cruise
guide		bruise
guard		nuisance
guinea		

* With **gu**, **gh**, the **u** and **h** are silent

u after g indicates an **unvoiced u**

e.g. **g**uide

55

eigh

eɪ

---

55   eight

This phonogram we call 'four letter **ā**'

weigh	sleigh
eight	eighteen
freight	neighbour

Exception: **height**

10
Awkward sounds and spellings: 'er', 'air' and 'ough'

This chapter shows phonograms that are most easily learnt by nonsense sentences:

These sentences may be written in chart form and similar spellings listed under each

er	ir	ur	ear	(w) or
her	bird	hurts	earth	worms
mother	first	turn	learn	word
fern	firm	burn	heard	work

Charts can also be made for other sounds which have more than one spelling, such as the 'air' sound:

where's	their	rare	bear's	lair
there	heir	mare	tear	hair
bare	stare	be ware	care less	share
de clare	com pare	Clare	pre pare	fan fare
air	stair	des pair	mil lion aire	chair
re pair	air lin er	fair	bairn	arm chair

82

ough

This phonogram has *six sounds* — they are most easily learned through a nonsense sentence.

Alth<u>ough</u> weak thr<u>ough</u> a r<u>ough</u> c<u>ough</u> still he f<u>ough</u>t the dr<u>ough</u>t.

There are only about 20 'ough' words in general use in the whole language.

| though | through | rough | cough | fought | drought |
| dough | throughout | enough | through | ought | plough |

N.B. Thorough is a variant of through.

11
Spelling units 56-58

56

The five spellings of the er sound

3

56 The five spellings of the er sound

These are often learned by a nonsense sentence.
Write the words across the double page of an exercise book and list similar spellings below as you come across them.

her	bird	hurts	earth	worms
fern	first	burn	earn	worse

Try adding these yourself:

exercise, turn, learn, firm, earnest, worth, purse, world, purchase etc.

Don't forget to write your own sentences with each new word that you learn.

57

The five spellings of the air sound

ɛə

57 The five spellings of the air sound

These spellings can be learned by a nonsense sentence.
Write the words across the double page of an exercise book and list similar spellings below as you come across them.

Where's their rare bear's lair?

Here are some words to list:
hair, pear, heir, there, stare, wear, dare, stairs, care, fair*, fare*

* Note: when you have two or more words which sound the same but have different spellings they are called homophones.

58 The six sounds of the phonogram ough

This phonogram can say six sounds

$\bar{o}$ $\overline{oo}$ uff   off   aw   ow
though through rough cough fought drought

Though weak through a rough cough still he fought the drought.

Write these words across the double page of an exercise book and list similar words underneath.

Some words to list: **enough, trough, dough, plough, bought**.
There are no more than about 20 in common use.

thorough is an old form of **through**

THE FAMILY CIRCUS By Bil Keane

"Know what, Mummy? 'Mrs.' sure isn't spelled like it sounds."

12
Some foreign spellings

This section examines words that have come into the language from another source, often with the spelling unaltered but with English pronunciation.

French	*Italian*	*German*	*Spanish*
chassis	pizza	kindergarten	matador
chef	spaghetti	hamburger	patio
fete	terracotta	frankfurt(er)	guitar
litre	pasta	waltz	stampede
louvre	soprano	zinc	mosquito
quiche	macaroni	rucksack	goanna
blancmange	volcano		alligator
cul-de-sac	balcony		chocolate
	casino		hurricane
	fiasco		cannibal
	arcade		

Chinese	*Persian*	*Arabic*	*Japanese*
wok	khaki	admiral	hibachi
typhoon	shawl	cotton	kimono
shanghai	crimson	zero	judo
		giraffe	

Dutch	*Portuguese*	*African languages*	*Turkish*
busy	verandah	safari	kiosk
cruise	emu	savannah	angora

Some foreign spellings

Cont'd.

Dutch	Portuguese	African languages	Turkish
deck	port (wine)	trek	sherbet
freight		chimpanzee	yoghourt
reef			
yacht			

American Indian	Aboriginal Australian	Finnish
tepee	galah	sauna
moccasin	brolga	
kayak	dingo	
	burramundi	
	billabong	
	kangaroo	

Eskimo	Indian
anorak	bungalow
igloo	curry
	polo
	chutney
	yoga
	dinghy

It might be fun to find out where the following words come from:

mandarin	pasteurised	scuba
flak	ack-ack	smog
diesel	aardvark	radar
laser	smorgasbord	pekinese

There are no phonograms for this section, as they are not strictly English, but *adopted* or *made-up* words. Words with foreign spellings make up a very small percentage of the language. They do not follow the rules of English spelling.

Write these words, noting peculiarities in spelling and practise using them in spoken and written sentences.

One way to learn an unusual spelling is to write down the word, marking the unusual feature(s).

spag<u>h</u>etti (English words do not end with i)

pizza   kayak   chassis
galah   apartheid

Now that the student has been trained to examine each letter in a word, anything unusual will stand out and will be easy to remember.

These words will no longer be a worry if they are examined and irregularities noted and if the student makes a point of using them in speech and writing. This way we make words 'our own'.

13
Spelling unit 59

59

Some Foreign Spellings

---

59 Some Foreign Spellings

Some words we have taken from other languages, retaining the original spelling

American
Indian: tepee, kayak, moccasin
French: fibre, tour, quiche, chassis
German: hamburger, frankfurt, kindergarten
Portuguese: verandah, emu
Spanish: matador, patio
Italian: piano, pizza, soprano, spaghetti
Turkish; kiosk
Australian: billabong, galah, kangaroo

14
Examples, dictation exercises, and homophones

The following pages, 90-96, contain lists for reading and dictation practice.

1. The second sound of c — used before e, i or y, pronounced s.

ice	cent	cit y	cy clone
face	of fice	a cid	fan cy
nice	cen tre	de cide	bi cyc le
fence	em brace	re cite	*cym bal

   N.B. ei after c, see p. 92.
           * Greek origin, see p. 110.

2. The second sound of g — used before e, i or y pronounced j.

gem	gin	*gyp sy
age	gin ger	gym nast
dun geon	gir affe	en er gy
dan ger	en gine	bi ol o gy

3. Other pronunciations for ch.

   (a) as K (school)

school	chlor ine	psy che	char ac ter
chord	stom ach	schol ar	chol er a
ache	chem ist	chron ic	Christ o pher
e cho	chor us	mech an ic	tech ni cal

Examples, dictation exercises, and homophones 91

(b)   as sh (chef)

chef	chas sis	sche dule	pa ra chute
chic	sa chet	chiv al ry	Chev ro let
niche	mach ine	cham pagne	char la tan
cache	char ade	pan ache	av a lanche

Words from Middle English Phonograms

1. ee — always in a stressed syllable.

bee	deed	jeep	spleen
see	peel	steel	sneeze
free	greet	wheel	ag ree
week	feed	sleep	re fu gee

2. ea — 3 sounds as in eat, bread, steak.

(a)
eat	each	speak	near ly
lead	team	dream	ea sy
leak	peach	please	en treat

(b)
bread	dead	wealth	read y
head	thread	health	wea ther
deaf	tread	breath	plea sure
threat	sweat	spread	*en dea vour

                * suffix our see p. 110.

(c)   steak   great   break

3. oa as in boat.

boat	loaf	float	shoal
goat	coast	throat	coast er
moan	soak	coax	toast er
toad	soap	groan	cock roach

4. oo two sounds as in tōol and hŏok

(a)
boot	mood	loose	bal loon
soon	cool	shoot	after noon
roof	spoon	bloom	*ty phoon
hoop	stool	snooze	*cock a too

                * Not English.

(b)
good	cook	rook	un der stood
wool	wood	brook	wood en
look	foot	shook	un der took

5. ar — as in car.

car	barn	var nish	Mars
bar	hard	bar ber	car di gan
art	carve	har ness	par tic le
part	charm	par don	har mon y

6. (a) ai — never used at the end of a word.

aid	vain	sail or	main tain
paid	train	dais y	com plain
tail	aim	dai ly	sus tain
rain	claim	fail ure	en ter tain

    (b) ay — used at the end of a word.

say	stray	dis play	Sun day
may	play	de lay	hoo ray
hay	clay	birth day	hol i day

7. (a) oi — never used at the end of a word.

oil	noise	a noint	oint ment
coin	moist	ap point	*bois ter ous
voice	point	poi son	em broi der

    * ous see p. 93.

    (b) oy — used at the end of a word.

oy!	ploy	en joy	en joy ment
boy	*buoy	des troy	*buoy ant
toy	Roy	an noy	em ploy ment

    * Silent u.

8. (a) ei — never used at the end of a word, pronounced as ee.

(only after c)	(as long a)	now shortened to short i or **schwa** sound (from French)
ceil ing	vein	foreign
re ceive	reins	sovereign
de ceive	reign	
con ceive	feint	

    N.B. For eigh words see p. 95.

(b) ey — used at the end of a word.

Pronounced as ee		as ay
key	hon ey	grey
mon ey	jock ey	they
mon key	kid ney	sur vey
vol ley	hock ey	con vey

9. (a) au — never used at the end of a word.

Pronounced as short ŏ

pause	haunt	trau ma	Aus tra li a
paunch	gauze	saun ter	saus age
fault	vault	au di ence	be cause
cause	launch	au thor	cau li flow er

* N.B. for augh words see p. 95.

(b) aw — can be used at the end of a word.

saw	yawn	bawl	brawl
paw	lawn	thaw	trawl er
draw	straw	flaw	draw er
hawk	shawl	claw	law yer

10. (a) ou — never used at the end of a word, prounced as in cow.

out	house	bounce	bound ar y
loud	cloud	mouth	com pound
sound	ground	lounge	moun tain
round	flour	bounce	trous ers

(b) ou — pronounced short u as in touch or as schwa in 'ous'.

touch	nour ish	fam ous	*re lig ious
cous in	cour age	*gor geous	glor i ous
count ry	south ern	vi cious	con scious
troub le	doub le	an xious	in fec tious

* e or i is required after g to make the j sound.

(c) Other pronunciations for ou.

as in or	oō as in boot	ō as in cold
pour	you	soul
four	soup	mould
your	group	poul try
course	youth	shoul der

11. (a) ow — can be used at the end of a word.

ow!	cow	gown	en dow	bow er
now	town	clown	tow el	tow er
how	brown	frown	trow el	flow er
vow	down	crowd		bow ser

(b)
sow (seed)	slow	pil low	to mor row
low	know	be low	o ver grown
tow	flow	win dow	brig a low
mow	glow	har row	stow a way

12. (a) eu — never used at the end of a word.

feud	neu tral	pleu ri sy
deuce	neu ter	rheu mat ism
sleuth	feu dal	neu rot ic

(b) ew — used at the end of a word.

new	blew	stew	stew ard
few	flew	drew	news reel
dew	knew	screw	cur lew
chew	grew	view	in ter view

More Examples

Less common forms can be taught as special lessons.

1. gn — two letter n.

   At the beginning of a word   At the end of a word
   (from Early English)   (from French)

gnaw	gnat	sign	for eign
gnash	gnarl	reign	mal ign
gnome		deign	cam paign

   N.B. When an ending beginning with a vowel is added to a word ending with gn, the two letters are sometimes sounded separately:

   sig na ture   mal ig nant   sig nal   sig ni fi cant

2. gn — u shows g must be hard, as in **get**.
   Usually at the beginning of a word.

guide	guest	guilt	guer il la
guard	guess	gui nea	gui tar
guar di an	van guard		

3. ui — pronounced 'o͞o' as in boot.

suit	bruise	nui sance
fruit	cruise	suit ab le
juice	sluice	jui cy

4. ie — pronounced as in pie.

As ī	Also ee as in piece		
pie	piece	niece	be lief
die	field	shield	re lief
lie	grief	brief	a chieve
tie	thief	priest	hand ker chief

5. igh — three letter i.

high	right	plight	de light
night	fight	fright	might y
thigh	light	slight	right eous
sigh	bright	knight	light ning

6. eigh.

| weigh | sleigh | neigh bour |
| eight | freight | weigh bridge |

7. augh.

Pronounced as 1. au in taut   2. as arf

| caught | haugh ty | laugh |
| taught | daugh ter | draught |

Homophones

Because English has derived words from so many different sources, there is an exceptional number which sound the same but are spelt differently and have different meanings.

e.g. weak comes from the old English word **wāc**
week comes from the Danish word **week**

Clue words can be used to show the difference in meaning and students should be encouraged to write their own sentences using the words.

e.g.	so	here	need	blue	
	sew (stitch)	hear (ear)	knead (bread)	blew (wind)	
	no	seem	witch	reed	steal
	know	seam	which	read	steel
	some	hair	pair	pale	mare
	sum	hare	pear	pail	mayor

Section 4

English words from Latin and Greek: how to understand and spell them

15. How to understand words built from Latin and Greek sources

16. Spelling units 60-63

17. Prefixes and suffixes
Word building
Examples and exercises

15
How to understand words built from Latin and Greek sources

These are the phonograms described in this chapter. They occur in words derived from Greek and Latin roots. They are detailed on pp. 103-104.

ti	ph	sc	pn
si	rh	eu	pt
ci			ps

This third group of words, formed by adding a syllable (or two, or more) to the beginning or end of a word *root*, is the most interesting of all.

These are the more flexible and sophisticated words, and when students understand them their vocabulary expands and they find it far easier to express themselves on a variety of subjects.

But it would be unwise to tackle these words until the student is fairly confident in the use of the English Base Words and knows most of the two, three and four letter phonograms of the Middle English and Invasion Words.

Phonograms (Latin and Greek)

1. ci, si and ti say **sh** at the beginning of a suffix-syllable. See p. 106.

    (a) Mostly if the base word has **c** (e.g. **face**) we use **ci**.

fa cial	fi nan cial	mu si cian
so cial	of fi cial	ar ti fi cial
spe cial	de li cious	com mer cial

    (b) Mostly if the base word has **s** and in 'mission' words, we use **si**.

man sion	pas sion	mis sion	pro gres sion
pen sion	ses sion	com mis sion	pro fes sion
ten sion	per mis sion	sub mis sion	con cus sion

    (c) Mostly if the base word has **t**, we use **ti**.

na tion	tor ren tial	con tra dic tion
sta tion	po ten tial	in ter rup tion
trac tion	col lec tion	su per sti tious

    (d) ti always follows **a** for noun ending **ation** meaning **act or state of**.

sta tion	e la tion	sep ar a tion
re la tion	mu ta tion	com bin a tion
dic ta tion	tax a tion	con ver sa tion

    (e) si after a vowel pronounced **zh** as in **vision**.

vi sion	oc ca sion	col lu sion
fu sion	di vi sion	per sua sion

    (f) Mostly **ian** for people as classification, **ion** for things.

mu si cian	Aus tra lian	in ven tion
phy si cian	pol it i cian	des crip tion

How to understand words built from Latin and Greek sources 101

NOTE: k sound before t *is* always spelt c.

    act   sec tion   pro duct   con duct or
    sect   fic tion   punc ture   con tra dict

2. ph pronounced as f.

    graph   tro phy   el e phant
    phone   phon ics   em pha tic
    phase   pho to graph   ge og raph y

rh pronounced as r.

    rhyme   rheu mat ism
    rhythm   rhi no cer os
    rhu barb   rho do den dron

3. sc pronounced as s in **scene**.

    scene   scis sors   scep tic
    scent   ab scess   de scent
    sci ence   as cend   ob scene

eu prounounced as ū.

    feud   eu cal yp tus
    Eu rope   pneu ma tic
    neu tral   pseu do

4. pn pronounced as n.

    pneu ma tic
    pneu mo ni a

pt pronounced as t.

    pto maine
    pte ro dac tyl
    ptar mi gan

ps pronounced as **s**.

        psalm
        pseu do
        psy chol o gy
        pso ri a sis
        psy che del ic

16
Spelling units 60-63

60

ti

si

ci

ʃ

---

60 ti si ci

These three phonograms all say **sh**.

We must use one of these when we hear the sh sound at the beginning of a syllable in the middle of a word — a word made up of Greek or Latin root to which we've added a suffix or ending.

ti	si	*	ci
nation	session	vision	social
fiction	mission	division	racial
relation	concussion	invasion	crucial
condition	tension	confusion	financial

* **si** may say **zh** as in **vision**

61

ph

rh

f r

---

61 ph rh

These two phonograms are from Greek

ph says **f**
phantom phonetic
elephant photograph
trophy telephone

rh the **h** is silent
rheumatic rhubarb
rhyme rhapsody
rhythm rhinoceros

103

62   sc says s when followed by e, i, y.

scene	scissors
scent	science
descent	scintillate
obscene	scythe

eu says $\bar{u}$ Europe
feud
neutral
eucalyptus

63   pn pt ps

Some unusual spellings from Greek

pn says n   **pt** says t
pneumatic   ptomaine
pneumonia   pterodactyl
                       ptarmigan

ps says s
psalm
pseudo
psychic
psychology

17
Prefixes and suffixes: word building, examples and exercises

To benefit fully from the instruction in this section it is helpful to have some knowledge of grammar. At the time of printing, a *Companion Grammar* is in production.

A noun is a thing — it exists whether you can see it or not. e.g. **glory**.
An adjective describes something e.g. **pretty**.
An adverb tells how something is done e.g. **nicely**.
A verb denotes action or being or having.

1. **Prefixes**

First, let us understand the use of a prefix — something fixed in front of (**pre** means **before**).

The prefix changes or adds to the meaning of the word root. For example, **un im** and **dis** can change the meaning of a word to the opposite (negative meaning).

tie	—	untie	fair	—	unfair
proper	—	improper	take	—	mistake
cover	—	discover	prove	—	disprove

re can mean back or again

turn	—	return	vise	—	revise
tread	—	retread	mem	—	remember
vive	—	revive	volve	—	revolve

105

Suffixes

1. Now let us see what happens to a word when we put a suffix at the end: *something fixed after*

   The suffix changes the word from one part of speech to another. That is, it changes its function — the part it plays — in the sentence.

   ness added to an *adjective* (a describing word) changes it to a *noun* (a thing).

   > **good** (adjective) becomes **goodness** (noun)

   -ly added to an *adjective* changes it to an *adverb* (a word that adds meaning to the *verb*.)

   > **bad** (adjective) becomes **badly** (adverb)

2. Sometimes spelling changes when we add a suffix. For example, in English we prefer not to have y in the middle of a word, so we change it to i.

   > tidy   tid<u>i</u>ness
   > heavy   heav<u>i</u>ly
   > muddy   mudd<u>i</u>er

   but we cannot do this if it causes two i's to come together.

   > try   try<u>i</u>ng

   or two vowels (which could form a misleading phonogram)

   > dry   dryest

Adding prefixes and suffixes to word roots

Let's take a root like **ject**, derived from a Latin word **throw**. From that we can make many new words by the addition of prefixes and suffixes.

First let us add prefixes:

> e   — ject   =   throw out of
> in   — ject   =   throw into
> re   — ject   =   throw back
> sub   — ject   =   throw under
> ob   — ject   =   throw against
> pro   — ject   =   throw forward

Now let us add some suffixes to those words:

prefix	root	suffix		
e	ject	or	=	that which throws out (of a seat) (noun)
pro	ject	ile	=	object thrown forward (noun)
in	ject	ion	=	that which is thrown into (noun)
con	ject	ure	=	that which is thrown together (an idea) (noun)
tra	ject	ory	=	that which is thrown over (a curve)

More examples:

1. tract, meaning draw or pull

    tract or   at tract ive   tract ion
    sub tract ion   ex tract or   de tract

2. pose, meaning put or place

    ex pose   com pose   dis pos able
    re pose   ex pos i tion   de pose
    com pos i tion   sup pose
    re pos i tory

3. Some common prefixes (added before the root to add to, or develop meaning).

Prefix	Meaning	Example
con/com	together (with)	com press
de	away from	de part
ultra	beyond	ultra sound
anti	against	anti dote
post	after	post pone

4. Some common suffixes (added after the root to change the part of speech).

Suffix	Meaning	Example	Part of Speech
ment	quality/state of	content ment	noun
ful	full of	care ful	adjective
ly	in the manner of	quick ly	adverb
fy	make	mag ni fy	verb
ize	act accordingly/using	vis u al ize	verb

5. Suffixes change the part of speech.

   (a) *Adjective*　　*Adverb*　　　*Noun*
   　　kind　　　　kindly　　　kind ness
   　　tense　　　 tense ly　　 ten sion
   　　hope ful　　hope ful ly　hope ful ness

   (b) 　　*verb to noun*　　　　*noun to adjective*
   　　act　　　act ion　　　bene fit　bene fi cial
   　　in vent　in ven tion　hab it　　hab it u al
   　　place　　place ment　 duty　　　du ti ful

6. We use e or i before suffixes to keep second sound of c and g.

   (a)　　　　　　　　　　　　(b)
   　　change able　　　　spa cious
   　　gor geous　　　　　re place able
   　　ad van ta geous　　*her ba ceous

   　　　* ce becomes sh as ci

7. Here are some more word roots from which to build new words

   　　mit — send
   　　duc — lead
   　　port — carry
   　　spec — see or look at

As students learn to recognise and separate word roots, prefixes and suffixes, their vocabulary will expand and reading and understanding will improve rapidly — so will spelling because they will understand *how* the word is *made*.

Only by using these words can they feel 'at home' with them and appreciate their value in writing and conversation.

Com or con?

1. Joining prefixes.

   (a) Com before b and p.

   com bine　　com bat　　　com post　　com bus tion
   com pact　　com pass　　 com press　 com bin a tion
   com plex　　com ply　　　com pany　　com part ment

(b) Doubling with m.

com mence	com mo tion	com man do
com mit	com mu nion	com men ta tor
com mon	com mit tee	com mod it y

(c) Doubling with r and l.

cor rect	cor rec tion	col lect	col li er
cor rupt	cor re late	col lapse	col lec tion
cor rode	cor ri dor	col lar	col lu sion

(d) Doubling with n.

con nect	con nec tion
con nive	con noi seur (French)
con nate	con ni vance

(e) Becomes con before c, d, f, g, j, qu, s, t, v.

con cave	con vic tion	con se quence
con duct	con ges tion	con tin en tal
con fess	con quer or	con fis cate
con jure	con trac tor	con vey or

2. Other prefixes follow the same pattern.

im pulse	sym path y	im mac u late
in tact	sum mar y	ir ri ta ble
syn drome	il lu sion	il lus tri ous

Some Greek and Latin word roots

1. Common roots and meanings

root	meaning	root	meaning
spec	look (watch)	mem	remember
dic	speak	cede	give
graph	drawn	form	shape

root	meaning	root	meaning
por(t)	carry	scribe	write
ver(t)	turn	vis	see
phon	sound	path	feel

2. Words from the root spec.

as pect — what is seen when one looks
sus pect — look beneath

spect rum   a visual display — what you see
                e.g. when light passes through a prism
spec tacles   lenses to look through

3. Greek syllables containing y — say ĭ, short or long.

   N.B. English prefer the letter i in the middle of a word and y only at the end.

   (a) as short ĭ.

sys tem	syn the tic	cy nic	hys te ri a
sym bol	sy ca more	crys tal	bi cy cle
syr inge	my ster y	nymph	py ra mid

   (b) as long ī.

cy cle	dy na mite	hy phen	ly ce um
cy clone	dy na mo	hy per bo la	psy cho lo gy
cy press	dy nam ic	hy po der mic	psy chic

More endings

1. Common suffixes from Latin via French.

   (a) our — noun, suffix meaning 'quality of'.

hon our	flav our	splen dour
o dour	fer vour	par lour
arm our	har bour	sa viour

   (b) ure — noun, suffix meaning 'act of' or 'resulting from'.

pic ture	tor ture	struc ture
tex ture	mix ture	press ure
lec ture	cul ture	junc ture

   (c) ine — noun, suffix meaning 'thing to do with'.
   pronounced <u>een</u> sometimes pronounced with long i.

mar ine	vas el ine	val en tine
rou tine	gas o line	con cu bine
sar dine	nic o tine	col um bine

2. Doubling consonants when adding an ending beginning with a vowel to two syllable words.

Prefixes and suffixes: word building, examples and exercises 111

(a) If the word ends with a single short vowel before a consonant *and* the stress is on the second syllable, the consonant is doubled.

re mit tance	trans mit ter	re but tal
for got ten	re cur red	e mit ting
com mis sion	ad mit ting	em bed ded

For a full list of prefixes, suffixes, word roots and their meanings refer to *English Words from Latin and Greek: how to understand and spell them*, a Nutshell Product.

Further exercises for reading, dictation and word building for words of Latin or Greek origin

You may wish to use a dictionary for these exercises but try without a dictionary first.

1. Give meaning and then write a sentence for each of the following words.

    e.g. e ject — throw out
    A jet pilot can eject from his seat in an emergency

contradict	submerge	conduct	concord
irregular	impolite	flexible	ultramodern
supervise	predict	expire	postmortem

2. As contentment is the state of being content, explain the following.

joyless	coldness	tiredness	investment
kindness	perfection	evasion	advertise
gently	harmless	quotation	hopelessness

3. Give an alternative definition for the following.

    e.g. payment: something given which was owed.

payment	hostility	conference	intelligence
pension	tenderness	amicably	fragrant
semblance	conflagration	indefinite	valueless

112   *Spelling Made Easy*

4. Make a list of words from each of the following roots.

dic	vis	form	tele
trac	mit	path	ver(t)
mem	phon	pend	por(t)

5. Comment on the spelling and/or meaning of the following words e.g. sympathy: sym Greek meaning **together** plus **path** Greek meaning feel

sympathy = feel together with

construction   immeasurable   jauntily

THE FAMILY CIRCUS By Bil Keane

"My memory isn't as good as my forgettery."

Section 5

Appendices

1. How the voice is produced

2. The difference between vowels and consonants

3. Writing tips

4. Breaking words into syllables

5. The rules to observe in spelling English Base Words

6. Some extra help with spelling

Appendices

1. How the voice is produced

We have a strong muscle running across the body beneath the rib cage which plays a major role in controlling our breathing and speech. When the lungs are full of air this diaphragm muscle is pushed flat, but when we need air for speaking it moves to a curved position, pushing air up and out of the lungs. The floating ribs assist the process by pushing inwards. The stream of air thus forced up reaches the voice box and vibrates the vocal cords, thereby producing sound waves.

The sound waves travel upon a stream of air which, on reaching the mouth, is broken up into single sounds by swift movements of tongue, lips, teeth, jaws, and so on. These movements determine the shape of the mouth cavity which permits the production of distinctive sounds.

More detailed information about voice production may be obtained from books in the speech and drama section of most bookshops.

2. Difference between vowels and consonants

In order to spell the English Base Words it is vital to understand the difference between vowels and consonants.

The *vowels letters* are a, e, i, o, and u and sometimes y. Both w and y can form part of a vowel phonogram as in ow, ew, ay, ey. The *consonant letters* are all the other letters of the alphabet including w and y.

When we speak a vowel we do not stop the outgoing breath at any point; it flows uninterruptedly out of the mouth. When we speak a consonant, we stop the breath, or impede it in some way, and then release it. It is also helpful to understand the close relationship between 'soft' and 'hard' sounds, sometimes called 'whispered' or 'spoken' consonants. For example, p and b are formed in the mouth in exactly the same way, but b is given more breath and is voiced. It is therefore called the 'hard' sound.

The same applies to t and d, k and g, f and v, s and z, ch and j, and sh and zh (as in vision). This information will help students in listening for single sounds in words and it will lead to clearer speech.

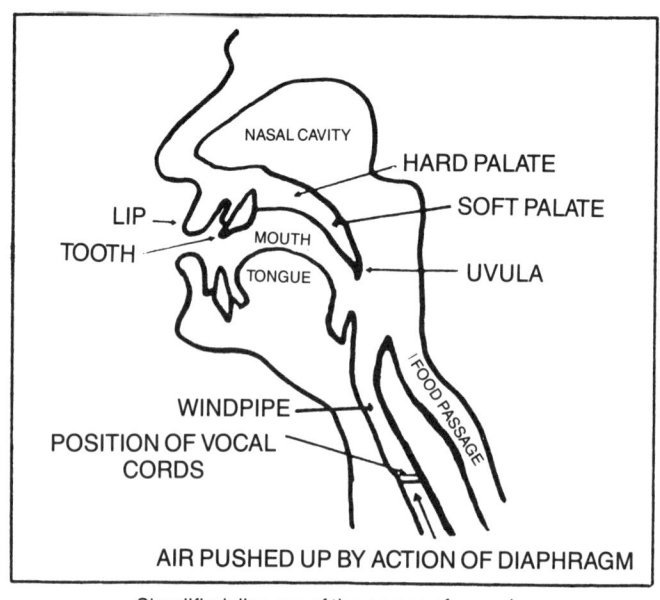

Simplified diagram of the organs of speech

Appendices 117

3. Writing tips

The Grip

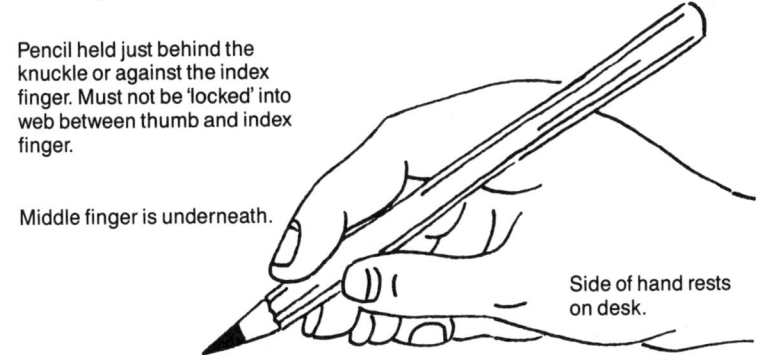

Pencil held just behind the knuckle or against the index finger. Must not be 'locked' into web between thumb and index finger.

Middle finger is underneath.

Side of hand rests on desk.

Leave 2 to 2.5 cm between the point of the pencil and the tip of the index finger so the writer can clearly see the pencil point. The fingers control the pencil. The hand and the arm move only to allow the writer to begin writing a new group of words.

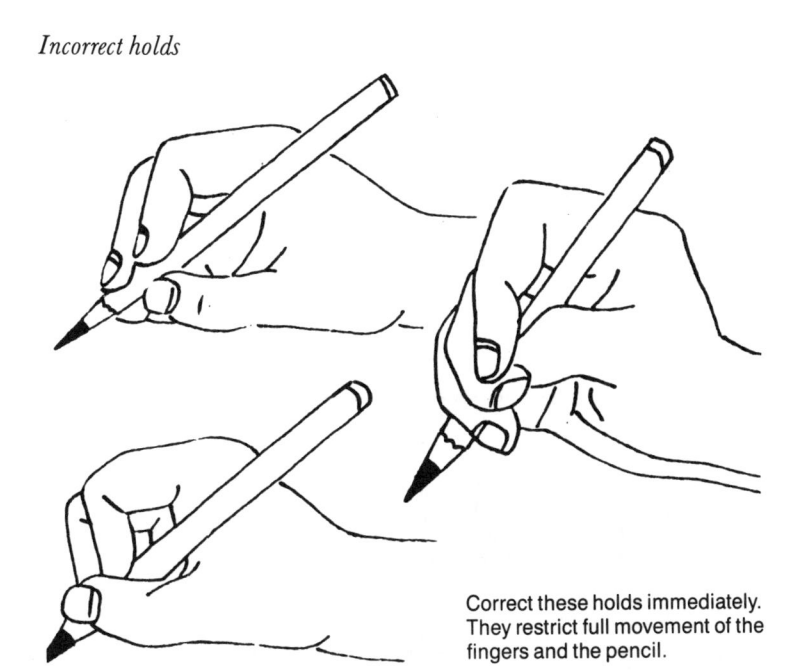

Incorrect holds

Correct these holds immediately. They restrict full movement of the fingers and the pencil.

Posture

The paper should be placed at about the same angle as the writing arm. The other hand holds the paper steady.

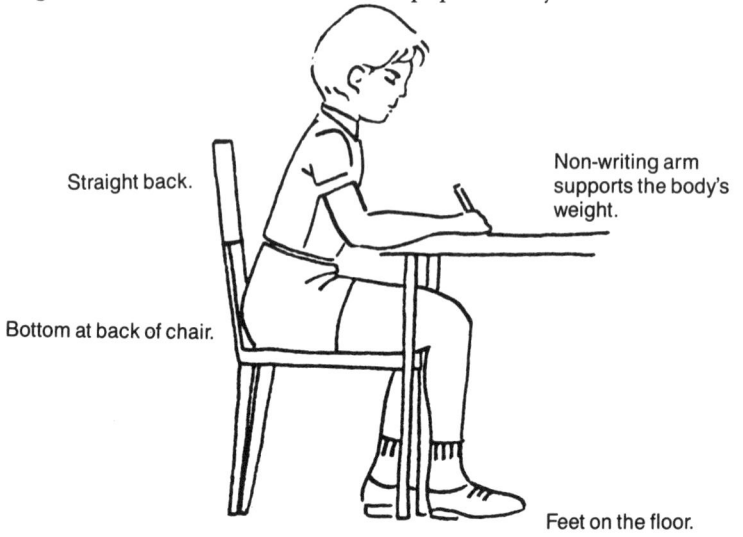

Straight back.

Non-writing arm supports the body's weight.

Bottom at back of chair.

Feet on the floor.

Lines

Children should write between the lines as soon as possible. They should be encouraged to form as much of the letter as possible without raising the pencil, until a separate stroke needs to be made. (See p. 26 for letter formation.)

Lines like these are the best for beginners.

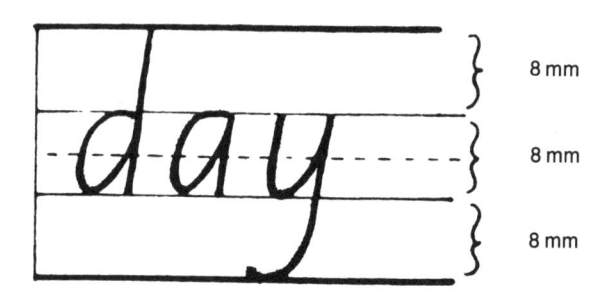

8 mm

8 mm

8 mm

4. Breaking words into syllables

It is vital to understand syllables in order to spell the lengthier words of the language.

A syllable is defined as 'that part of a word which is spoken with a single impulse of the voice'. Every syllable contains a vowel sound. The sound may be the neutral sound of 'schwa' which occurs frequently in English words. It is the *unstressed* sound in such words as the (not thee), mother, cathedral, enormous. The schwa sound is indicated by the symbol ǝ in dictionaries.

Note: When learning spelling we sound the vowel written in the syllable even though it is not pronounced fully in normal speech. For example, per man ent pronounced man — and the brain records it thus.

A good way for students to detect the number of syllables in a word is to count the number of times the lower jaw drops when the word is spoken. Put the back of the hand under the chin and each time a vowel sound is spoken the lower jaw will drop.

It is very important for a student to form the habit of mentally breaking words into syllables before attempting to spell them. (It will improve speech too! How many people say 'pleece' — one syllable — for 'police'?) When practising the day's 'spellings' from school, for instance, the words should first be written down in syllables thus:

    com bin a tion
    di al
    so ci et y
  * lit tle

---

* The neutral vowel occurs between the consonant and the letter 'l' in words of this type, even though the ǝ comes at the end of the word.)

5. The rules to observe in spelling English Base Words

1. Write only one letter for one sound unless you know a reason for adding an extra letter.

The reasons for adding an extra letter are as follows:

a. *The long vowel pattern.* Adding a vowel to make the previous vowel 'say its own name'.

> ta<u>pe</u>   h<u>o</u>me

b. *The short vowel pattern.* Adding another consonant to keep the preceding vowel short.

> stepping   hotter

c. When the k sound follows a short vowel which says ă, ĕ, ĭ, ŏ, ŭ in a base word it is spelt ck (if another consonant does not follow as in act).

d. When the ch sound follows a short vowel which says ă, ĕ, ĭ, ŏ, ŭ it is spelt tch.
   (There are five exceptions — much, such, which, rich, sandwich.)

e. When j sound follows a short vowel sound which says ă, ĕ, ĭ, ŏ, ŭ it is spelt dge.

> badge   fudge

f. We often double f, l, s, z after the five short vowels.

> stiff   bill   miss   buzz

A few special features:

1. The k sound is written with the letter c in front of a consonant or in front of a, o, u.

> cat   cot   cut

2. The k sound is written with the letter k in front of e or i; also after a long vowel sound.

> kettle,   kitchen,   break

3. Some pecularities about u and v
   a. We do not double v in English words except in some slang words — flivver, navvy, revving, skivvy.
   b. The short vowel sound ŭ is often spelt with o before v.

   love   dove   glove   shove   above

6. Some extra help with spelling

e at the end of a word

1. **e** makes the previous vowel long

       māte   whīle   rōpe

2. **e** is used after **c** to denote the **s** sound, and after **g** to denote the **j** sound.

       force   large

   (for rule see p. 74)

3. In English, **i**, **u** and **v** are never found at the end of words — **e** is always added.

       give   tie   blue

4. In words like **mud/dle**, **rip/ple**, **ta/ble** there are two syllables and, since every syllable must have a vowel, we add **e** to the second one.

5. In some words we still have an **e** which formerly had a purpose, but no longer has.

       some   are   done

6. If an ending beginning with a vowel is added to a base word ending with **e**, then the **e** must be dropped.

       write   writing

   (*Exception:* The **e** is retained if **e** has another job to do — for example, to show that **g** has the sound of **j** as in **manageable**.)

C and g

1. The letter **c** says **s** if it is followed by **e**, **i** or **y**.

       cell   Cinderella   cycle

2. If the letter **g** comes before **e**, **i** or **y**, it *may* say **j**.

       gem   giant   gym

   (*Exceptions:* **get, got, give** — being English Base Words.)

Sh sound

1. If the 'sh' sound is at the beginning of a suffix, it is spelt **ti, si** or **ci**.

    rela<u>ti</u>on   ten<u>si</u>on   fa<u>ci</u>al

    (*Exception:* **cushion, fashion** [French])

More spelling tips

1. **a, e, o, u** usually have their long sound at the end of a syllable.

    mō tel   lā ter   sō

2. The letters **i** and **o** often have the long sound before two consonants.

    fīnd, wīld, cōld (no final **e** is required)

3. The ŏ sound after **w, wh** and **qu** is often spelt with an **a**.

    was   wander   what   squat   quarrel

4. If we add **all, full** or **fill** to other words we drop one **l**.

    always   awful   fulfil.   Also until

A final word

Phonic and Sight Skills must be developed in unison.

It is important to understand the relationship between the teaching of English phonetically and sight-word reading.

There is no such thing as phonics *in isolation*. Sight words are learnt by seeing them often enough for them to be remembered. The formation of individual letters is partly learnt this way too; memory skills must be involved in any learning operation.

Memory is the kingpin of all learning, so the training of memory skills is the foundation of education — the learning how to learn.

The brain is a computer of infinite storage and reasoning power. Both functions must be fed, trained and exercised for results to be produced. The more sensory skills — or channels into the mind — we use in training memory and reason, the more competent those functions will become.

Children learning by phonics to sound out the word 'hop' will have to see the word only the same number of times as children of similar ability learning to read by sight, for that word to become a sight word for them too. For them, the intervening period between when they see 'hop' for the first time and when they have seen it enough times to remember it presents no problem, because they can work it out for themselves; moreover, the advantage that phonics-trained children have is apparent when they are then presented with the word 'hog' and can work out the difference for themselves.

This book describes the drill for learning sounds and writing symbols. The importance of the association between seeing, hearing, speaking and writing cannot be over-emphasised. Thus the child who learns by sight methods only is, at this stage, significantly disadvantaged. For the child who is learning by phonics, both skills are, from the start, inseparably bound together and reinforce one another.

Most adults reading a novel sight read as much as 90 per cent of the words. **Experience in teaching older children and adults who have literacy problems shows that their phonic and sight skills have not been developed in unison.**

It is also true that sight reading can, by practice, develop a certain amount of phonic understanding. Thus a proportion of people who possess a naturally pictorial memory become good readers and spellers at school, without much phonic instruction. What they still lack is an understanding of the technical aspects of language structure and rules vitally important for advanced studies in any subject at all.

On the other hand, the student who does not have a pictorial memory finds it very difficult to memorise whole words by sight. *The type of memory bears no relationship to the degree of intelligence, and a non-pictorial memory often accompanies above average skill in mathematics and a need for a logical approach.*

Phonics instruction enables these children to work out for themselves each word as they come to it. From the first week at school they are learning to apply knowledge — the skill which is the basis of logical thinking.

Many studies have been carried out on so-called disadvantaged children; to discover why they have a lower standard of literacy than children from so-called advantaged backgrounds. From our experience and that of our colleagues, working with both remedial children and adults, we firmly believe that the problems of these children result entirely from their lack of both technical skills and the brain-training and exercise which accompany the development of these skills.

Children who are entirely dependent on their sight memory and cannot get help from home become increasingly frustrated and lose confidence in their own ability, and the child with these problems becomes an adult with more. These same children, if taught how to work out the word phonically, could apply this knowledge for themselves — they could then read on, decoding new words too. An exciting by-product of this situation is that the family responds to their new skills and in some cases starts learning too.

While undertaking a study in a special school, we came across exactly this situation among a number of children of different racial origins. They were still being taught by those same methods that had earlier failed them in school. There are frightening numbers of children and older students who suffer from similar literacy problems in varying degrees.

Our experience has shown that *no* children, however deprived their backgrounds, need be deprived of reading and writing skills. Moreover, the greater literacy advantage we can give them, the more successfully they will be able to lift themselves above the disadvantages of their environment.

We know that a phonics-first approach leads to happy and successful learning, and we dedicate this little book to all those students who gave us so much valuable experience and for whom we set down the methods and information in the first place.

Index

alphabetic writing 12
air spellings 82-83
Anglo Saxons 19
Celtic tongues 18
Christianity 20
com or con 108
compound words 68
consonants 36, 74
  combinations 30, 61
  definition of 116
  doubling 38, 39
curved letters 26
Danes 20, 21
doubling consonants 38, 39
English base phonograms 41-53
English Base Words 7, 15, 33-40
English Base Words for dictation 69
er spellings 82
foreign spellings 86-87
Greek and Latin derived words 16, 98-112
homophones 95-96
i changing to y 66-67
ideographic writing 11
Industrial Revolution 23
Latin and Greek derived words 16, 98-112
markings for spelling 30
Middle English including invasion words 7, 16, 71-96
Normans 21
ough words 82-83
parts of speech 105

past tense ending 59
phonogram cards
  English Base Words 41-53
  Greek and Latin derived words 104-105
  Middle English 76-81, 84-85, 89
phonic skills 125-127
pictographic writing 11
plurals 62
posture 118
prefixes 8, 17, 105-112
Romans and influence 18-20
roots, word roots 105-7, 109
rules for English Base Words 38, 120
schwa 8, 14, 69, 92, 119
silent e ending 31
  dropped 122
silent letters 68
stress (emphasis) 59, 64
suffixes 8, 17, 105-112
syllables
  definition 119
  breaking words 119
synonyms 21
Vikings 20
voice production 115
vowels
  definition 116
  short and long patterns 35, 36, 38-39, 56, 60, 75
  rules for long vowel pattern 38, 122
writing 28, 117